GEORGIA
FREE PERSONS
OF COLOR

Volume V
Richmond County
1799-1863

By
Michael A. Ports

CLEARFIELD

Reprinted for Clearfield Company by
Genealogical Publishing Company
Baltimore, Maryland
2016

ISBN 978-0-8063-5813-0

Table of Contents

Introduction

In 1818, the Georgia legislature enacted a law requiring free persons of color to register with the inferior court of the county of their residence. Registers survive for only twenty-one of Georgia's counties. While the law required the inferior court clerks to maintain registers with the names, ages, places of nativity, residence, time of coming into the state, and occupation of each free persons of color, an evaluation of the surviving registers reveals very little consistency in either format or information recorded between the various counties or even within a particular county over time. The following transcriptions include the four extant registers from Richmond County, made from the original records available at the Georgia Department of Archives and History, Morrow, Georgia.

Overall, the quality of the original records is good and the handwriting of the various court clerks is legible, making the transcription straightforward and not too difficult. However, ink blots, smears, clerks scribbling, as well as other imperfections, occasionally make transcribing the records problematic, such problems noted between brackets, for example [smudge] or [illegible]. The transcriptions follow Sperry's recommended guidelines for reading early American script.[1] Researchers should consult the original records, to either confirm the transcription or formulate alternative interpretations of the handwriting.

Because the four registers differ in both format and information recorded, subsequent chapters each include an introduction explaining the format and content of each transcription. Throughout the original registers, the various clerks made extensive use of both ditto marks and the letters "Do" or "do" to indicate a duplication of a previous entry, the following transcription repeating the previous entry in full. For consistency and to avoid confusion, the tabular transcriptions spell out the names of states, counties, and cities, regardless of how the names are abbreviated. Also, Georgia is not repeated after the names of counties located within the state. In a similar manner, the following full name index simplifies the suffixes Jr. and Sr., regardless of how they appear in the original record. Dates are presented in a consistent format, regardless of how they appear in the original. Occupations also are standardized. For example, blacksmith is preferred over black smith, blk smith, etc. All names are transcribed as accurately as possible, misspellings not corrected no matter how obvious the error.

A brief synopsis of the Georgia laws governing manumissions and the registration of free persons of color follows the Introduction. Also included is a list of the manumissions issued by the Georgia state legislature from 1799 to 1865. The full name index following the transcriptions of the four registers includes the names of all affiants, agents, clerks, guardians, justices, and free persons of color.

---

[1] Sperry, Kip, *Reading Early American Handwriting*. Genealogical Publishing Company, Inc., Baltimore, Maryland, Sixth Printing, 2008.

Many thanks are offered the very helpful and knowledgeable staff of the Georgia Department of Archives and History for their kind assistance and suggestions, not only in locating the records, but also in understanding their historical context. Thanks also are offered Joe Garonzik of the Genealogical Publishing Company for his professional advice and counsel. Special thanks are due Marcia Tremonti for her patience and encouragement through this challenging, but interesting endeavor.

Georgia Laws

The following presents a synopsis of the various Georgia laws governing slave manumissions and registration of free persons of color prior to 1837. The synopsis is not a comprehensive list of all of the provisions of all of the laws passed at different times, but rather is intended only to be a summary of the applicable laws. Researchers desiring a more detailed discussion of the laws should consult the work of W. McDowell Rogers.[2]

On December 5, 1801, Georgia enacted a law governing the manumission of slaves.[3] In part, the act provided

47. Sec. I. From and after the passing of this act, it shall not be lawful for any person or persons to manumit or set free any negro slave or slaves, any mulatto, mestizo, or any other person or persons of color, who may be deemed slaves at the time of the passing of this act, in any other manner or form, than by an application to the legislature for that purpose.

The Act of December 15, 1810 required all free persons of color to register with their local courts and provided for their guardianship.[4]

56. Sec. VII. The judge of the superior or the justices of the inferior courts of the respective counties of this State, shall, upon the written application of any free negro or person of color, made at any regular term of the said courts, praying that a white person resident of the county in which such application may be made, and in which such free person of color shall reside, may be appointed his or her guardian, appoint such white person the guardian of such free person of color. And the said guardian of such free negro or person of color, shall be, and is hereby vested with all the powers and authority of guardians for the management of the persons and estates of infants; and all suits necessary to be brought for or against such free person of color, shall be in the name of such guardian, in his capacity of guardian: Provided nevertheless, that the property of such guardian shall in no case be liable for the acts or debts of his ward.

57. Sec. VIII. The said judges of the superior or justices of the inferior courts shall at their discretion require security from such guardian as may be appointed, for the proper management of the affairs of his ward. And such guardian shall be allowed the same compensation for the discharge of his duties as guardian, as is allowed the guardians of infants by the laws of this State.

---

[2] Rogers, W. McDowell, *Free Negro Legislation in Georgia Before 1865.* The Georgia Historical Quarterly, Volume XVI, Number 1, March 1932, Page 27. Georgia Historical Society, Savannah, Georgia.

[3] Prince, Oliver H., *Digest of the Laws of the State of Georgia*, page 787. Athens, Georgia, 1837. (Hereinafter cited as Prince.)

[4] Prince, page 789.

On December 19, 1818, the legislature effectively replaced the Act of 1810.[5]

Whereas the principles of sound policy, considered in reference to the free citizens of this State, and the exercise of humanity towards the slave population within the same, imperiously require that the number of free persons of color within this State should not be increased by manumission, or by the admission of such persons from other States to reside therein; and *whereas* divers persons of color, who are slaves by the law of this State, having never been manumitted in conformity to the same, are nevertheless in the full exercise and enjoyment of all the rights and privileges of free persons of color, without being subject to the duties and obligations incident to such persons, thereby constituting a class of people, equally dangerous to the safety of the free citizens of this State, and destructive of the comfort and happiness of the slave population thereof, which it is the duty of this legislature by all just and lawful means to suppress:

93. Sec. III. From and after the passing of this act, it shall not be lawful for any free person of color, (Indians in amity with the State, and regularly articled seamen or apprentices, arriving in any ship or vessel, excepted,) to come into this State; and each and every person or persons offending herein, shall be liable to be arrested by warrant, under the hand and seal of any magistrate in this State, and being thereof convicted in the manner hereinafter pointed out, shall be liable to a penalty not exceeding one hundred dollars, and upon failure to pay the same within the time prescribed in the sentence awarded against such person or persons, he, she, or they, shall be liable to be sold by public outcry, as a slave or slaves, in such manner as may be prescribed by the court awarding such sentence, and the proceeds of such sales shall be appropriated in the manner provided for the appropriation of penalties recovered under this act.

95. Sec. V. All and every free person or persons of color, residing or being within this State, at the time of the passing of this act, and continuing or being therein on the first day of March next, except as hereinbefore excepted, shall, on or before that day, and annually on or before the first Monday in March in each and every succeeding year, which they shall continue to be within the limits of this State, make application to the clerk of the inferior court in the county in which they reside, and it shall be the duty of said clerk to make a registry of such free person or persons of color, in a book by him to be kept for that purpose, particularly describing therein the names, ages, places of nativity and residence, time of coming into this State, and occupation or pursuit of such free person or persons of color; and such clerk shall be entitled to demand and receive fifty cents for each and every person or persons so registered as aforesaid, and for granting a certificate thereof, which he shall in like manner be bound to do so on or before the first Monday in May thereafter, if no person shall appear to gainsay the same; and to the intent that all persons concerned or interested therein, may have due notice thereof, it shall be the duty of such clerk forthwith, after the said first Monday in March in each and every year, to cause to be published in one or more of the public gazettes of the county, or in counties where there are no gazettes, in

---

[5] Prince, page 794.

6

some one or more of the gazettes of the State, a list of such free persons of color, applying for registry, with notice that certificates will be granted to such applicants, if no objections are made thereto, on or before the second Monday in April thereafter; and each and every person desirous of objecting thereto, shall file such his objections in the office of such clerk within the time specified in such notice, which proceedings shall be by the said clerk notified to the justices of the inferior court of such county, and shall be tried and determined in the manner hereinafter pointed out; and the said clerk shall grant or withhold such certificate, according to the determination thereof: *Provided*, that the expense of such publication shall be defrayed out of the county funds, where the moiety of the several penalties prescribed by this act is appropriated to the county, and out of the funds of the city of Savannah where such moiety is appropriated to the corporation of the city.

96. Sec. VI. All and every person of color (Indians in amity with this State, or regularly articled seamen or apprentices arriving in any ship or vessel excepted) who shall, after the first Monday in May next, be found within the limits of this State, whose names shall not be enrolled in the book of registry, described in the preceding section, or having been enrolled, who shall have been refused certificates in the manner therein prescribed, and who shall be working at large, enjoying the profits of his or her labor, and not in the employment of a master or owner, or of some white person, by and in virtue of an actual and bona fide contract, with the master or owner of such person of color, securing to such master or owner the profits arising from the labor of such person of color, shall be deemed, held, and taken to be slaves, and may be arrested by warrant under the hand of any magistrate of this State, and such proceedings being had as are hereinafter provided, shall be sold by public outcry as slaves, and the proceeds of such sales shall be appropriated in the manner specified in the first section of this act.

On December 22, 1819, the legislature amended the Act passed the previous year.[6]

103. Sec. I. All free persons of color contemplated in the above-recited act, who failed to comply with the provisions therein contained, shall be, and they are hereby declared to be exonerated, released, and discharged from all pains or forfeitures to which they were thereby subjected; *Provided*, they do on or before the first Monday in July next, and annually thereafter on the first Monday in July, comply with the provisions contained in said act; *Provided*, that this act shall not extend to any case where there has been an actual forfeiture and sale.

106. Sec. IV. The above-recited act shall not extend to and operate upon free persons of color who are minors, and bound out according to law.

On December 20, 1824, Georgia passed *An Act to repeal all laws and parts of laws which authorize the selling into slavery of free persons of color.*[7]

---

[6] Prince, page 799.

On December 26, 1826, the legislature passed an act amending several provisions concerning free persons of color.[8]

113. Sec. II. Previous to the granting of certificates of registry of freedom, it shall be the duty of the clerks of the superior and inferior courts of the several counties of this State to give ten days' notice in one of the public gazettes, or in some other public manner, of the name of the applicant or applicants, his age, &c., and of his, or hers, or their guardian or guardians.

114. Sec. III. Such certificate of registry of freedom, when issued as aforesaid, shall contain an accurate description of the person, age, or occupation, and residence of such person of color, and that the clerk so issuing the same shall be entitled to have and receive from the guardian of such person of color the sum of five dollars; and should any free negro or person of color transfer his or her certificate of registry of freedom obtained as aforesaid to any slave, or free negro, or other person of color, such free negro or person of color so offending shall be punished by such fine, imprisonment, and other corporal punishment as any court competent to try slaves and free persons of color may in its discretion think proper to inflict.

On December 21, 1829, Georgia passed *An Act to amend the Acts concerning the Guardianship of Free Persons of Color.*[9]

120. Whereas, it frequently happens that the citizens of this State decline a permanent guardianship of free persons of color, by which the ends of justice are prevented; *Be it enacted, &c.* That from and after the passage of this act, free persons of color may exercise the right heretofore secured to them, of suing and being sued, pleading and being impleaded, answering and being answered unto, by the aid of a next friend as well as by a guardian.

121. Sec. II. Guardians of free persons of color shall have the privilege, with the consent of the inferior courts, of resigning their appointments at any time they wish to do Such.

On December 26, 1835, the Georgia legislature passed *An Act to amend the several laws now in force in relation to Slaves and Free Persons of Color.*[10]

163. Sec. I. *Be it enacted,* That from and after the passing of this act, it shall not be lawful for the clerk of any county in this State to register as free persons of color, or to grant a certificate of such registry to any person of color, who shall not establish by proof, to the satisfaction of the

---

[7] Prince, page 800.

[8] Prince, page 800.

[9] Prince, page 802.

[10] Prince, page 810.

8

inferior court of said county, that he or she, applying so to be registered, is *bona fide* and truly a free person of color, according to and under the laws of this State, or has been registered in this State, or has exercised all the privileges of a free person of color, for five years before the passing of this act. That it shall be the duty of such clerk to file in his office the evidence on which he shall grant such application, and that any clerk violating this law shall be guilty of a high misdemeanor, and on conviction shall be subject to a fine of three hundred dollars, to be paid one half to the informer, the other half to county purposes.

164. Sec. II. From and after the first day of June next, it shall not be lawful for any person of color, other than a slave, or a free person of color duly admitted to register in manner aforesaid, to remain in this State; and if any free person of color, other than as aforesaid, shall be found in this State after the said first day of June next, he or she shall be arrested and tried, and if convicted of a violation of this law, he or she shall pay a fine of $100, and in default of such payment, it shall be lawful for the court to bind them out as laborers until the fine is paid by the hire of such labor, and shall moreover be liable and subject to a repetition of such conviction, fine and punishment, at the end of thirty days after any such conviction and payment of such fine, until he or she shall actually depart this State, and that it shall be the duty of such [each] and every civil officer of this State to carry into effect his law.

165. Sec. III. From and after the passage of his law, it shall not be lawful for any free person of color who shall leave this State, other than to go to an adjoining State, again to return to it; and any and every free person of color entitled under the laws of this State to registry, who shall after the passage of this law go out of this State to any place other than to an adjoining State, for a temporary or other purpose, he or she, so leaving this State, shall thereby forfeit and lose his or her rights to registry as aforesaid, and all rights to reside in this State, and if thereafter found in this State, he or she shall be dealt with and subject to the pains and penalties described in the second section of this act.

170. Sec. VIII. The inferior courts of the several counties in this State shall have power and discretion to refuse and deny to any free person of color of bad character the right to register his or her name; and such free person of color shall then, after such refusal, be deemed and held a free person of color in this State in violation of this law, and be liable and subject to the pains and penalties herein prescribed.

Manumissions

Because the official policy of Georgia was to discourage and limit manumissions, the state legislature issued very few during the ante bellum period. The following acts of the legislature manumitting slaves, from 1798 through 1865, are from the database of legislative acts available on the Georgia Department of Archives and History website. Because the database, while substantial, is not complete, some additional acts of manumission may be missed. Supplemental information concerning the manumissions, including the original petitions, could survive in the State legislative records held by the archives. The full titles of the acts appear in italics.

Acts of the General Assembly of the State of Georgia: Passed at Louisville, in January and February, 1799. Vol. 1, Page 148. Sequential Number: 035.

An act to manumit and exempt from certain penalties, Silvia, and her son David, now the property of Joseph Gabriel Posner.

WHEREAS Joseph Gabriel Posner, hath by his petition presented to this present General Assembly, prayed that Silvia, a woman of color, and David her son, the property of the said Joseph Gabriel Posner, should be manumitted and discharged from slavery:

Sec. 1. Be it enacted by the Senate and House of Representatives of the State of Georgia, in General Assembly met, That from and after the passing of this act the said Silvia and David shall be and they are hereby declared to be manumitted and made free, and be thereafter utterly, clearly and fully discharged from slavery, as if the said Silvia and David had been born free.

Sec. 2. And be it further enacted, That if it shall so happen that the said Silvia or David should be charged or accused of any offence or crime whatsoever, the said Silvia or David shall be tried for such offence, in the same manner, and be entitled to the same defense, in the courts of this state, as allowed to free white persons in like cases.

Approval Date: Assented to February 9, 1799.

Acts of the General Assembly of the State of Georgia: Passed at Louisville, in January and February, 1799. Vol. 1, Page: 23. Sequential Number: 049

Acts of the General Assembly of the State of Georgia: Passed at Louisville, in November and December, 1799. Augusta: Printed by John E. Smith, Printer to the State. MDCCC.

An Act to manumit certain persons therein named.

Whereas James King, late of the city of Charleston, deceased, did by his last will and testament, bearing date the twenty-sixth day of March, in the year of our Lord one thousand seven hundred and ninety-seven, direct his executors therein named "to take care of and manumit, as soon as possible, his two negroes Lewis and China."

And Whereas Alexander King and Joshua Moore, the executors named in the said last will and testament of the said James King, have by petition applied to the present legislature, praying that the benevolent intentions of the said James King towards the said negroes be carried into effect:

Sec. 1. Be it therefore enacted by the Senate and House of Representatives of the State of Georgia in General Assembly met, That the said negroes Lewis and China be, and they are hereby manumitted and made free, and they are hereby entitled to the same privileges and immunities as if they had been born free.

And Whereas Ezekiel Hudnall has by his petition prayed the legislature to manumit the following slaves: Bridget Waters and her children, Leviny, Nancy, Daniel, and Syrus.

Sec. 2. Be it enacted, That the said Bridget, Leviny, Nancy, Daniel, and Syrus shall be, and they are hereby declared to be free and manumitted according to the prayer of the said petition.

And Whereas it appears to this present general assembly that a certain Harry M'Clendon, formerly the property of Jacob M'Clendon, and Rose his wife, formerly the property of Andrew M'Lean, have purchased their freedom, together with the freedom of their children, of and from their former owners, and have prayed that their freedom, as purchased, be secured by law.

Sec. 3. Be it further enacted, That the said Harry, Rose and their children Betsy and Kesiah, be and they are hereby declared to be free.

Sec. 4. Provided always, and be it further enacted, That nothing in this act contained shall be construed to give any person herein manumitted, any privileges except such as free people of color are entitled to by the laws of this state.

Approval Date: Assented to December 5, 1799.

Acts of the General Assembly of the State of Georgia Passed at Louisville, in November and December, 1801. Vol. 1, Page 40. Sequential Number: 015.

An Act to manumit and make free certain persons of colour, whose names are therein mentioned.

Whereas Richard Meriwether, and others, have petitioned the present Legislature, praying that, an Act may be passed, to manumit and make free Lucy Barrot, and Betty Barrot, Jim, commonly called Jim Lary, and a mulatto girl, named Nancy, late the property of Alexander Kevan, persons of colour, who are their right and property.

11

Sec. 1. Be it therefore enacted by the Senate and House of Representatives of the State of Georgia, in General Assembly met, and by the authority of the same, That Lucy Barrot, and Betty Barrot, Jim, commonly called Jim Lary, late the property of John B. Lary, and mulatto girl named Nancy, late the property of Alexander Kevan, persons of colour, be and they are hereby manumitted, and made free, and entitled to the same rights, privileges and immunities, as if they were born free.

Sec. 2. Be it further enacted, That this Act, shall not be so construed as to give, or grant unto the aforesaid Lucy Barrot, and Betty Barrot, Jim, commonly called Jim Lary, late the property of John B. Lary, and a mulatto girl named Nancy, late the property of Alexander Kevan, persons of colour, who do appertain to the household of Richard Meriwether, and others and who are hereby manumitted and made free, any rights, privileges, or immunities, except such as free people of colour, are entitled to by the laws of this state.

Sec. 3. And be it further enacted by the authority aforesaid, That the aforesaid persons of colour, who are hereby manumitted and made free, shall nevertheless be subject and liable to any legal demands which now doth exist, against the aforesaid Richard Meriwether, and others.

Approval Date: Assented to December 1, 1801.

Acts of the General Assembly of the State of Georgia Passed in Milledgeville at an Annual Session, in November and December, 1831. Vol. 1, Page: 225. Sequential Number: 174.

An Act to be entitled an act to manumit and set free from slavery Sophia, a person of colour, the property of Eli Fenn, and to give her a name.

Be it enacted by the Senate and House of Representatives of the State of Georgia, in General Assembly met, and it is hereby enacted by the authority of the same, That from and after the passage of this act, Sophia, a person of colour, now the property of Eli Fenn, shall be manumitted and set free from slavery, and shall be entitled to all the rights, immunities, and privileges, as though she had been born free.

Sec. 2. And be it further enacted by the authority aforesaid, That in future the said Sophia shall be called and known by the name of Sophia Fenn.

Approval Date: Assented to Dec. 19, 1831.

Acts of the General Assembly of the State of Georgia Passed in Milledgeville at an Annual Session, in November and December, 1833. Vol. 1 -- Page: 289. Sequential Number: 133.

An Act to manumit and set free Mary, a woman of colour, and her child Cordelia, now the property, wife and child of Lovewell C. Fluellin, a free man of colour.

12

Be it enacted by the Senate and House of Representatives of the State of Georgia, in General Assembly met, and it is hereby enacted by authority of the same, That from and after the passing of this act, Mary, a woman of colour, and her child Cordelia, now the property, wife and child, of Lovewell C. Fluellin, a free man of colour, shall be manumitted and set free, from slavery, and shall be entitled to all the rights, immunities, and privileges, as though she and her child Cordelia had been born free.

Approval Date: Assented to 24th Dec. 1833.

Acts of the General Assembly of the State of Georgia Passed in Milledgeville at an Annual Session, in November and December, 1834. Vol. 1, Page: 230. Sequential Number: 173.

An Act to manumit and set free certain persons therein mentioned.

Sec. 1. Be it enacted by the Senate and House of Representatives of the State of Georgia in General Assembly met, That from and after the passage of this act, Fanny Hickman, who is, and has been for more than thirty years, the wife of Paschal Hickman of the county of Burke, shall be, and she is hereby declared to be free, and entitled to all the privileges and immunities appertaining to free persons of colour generally in this State.

And whereas the said Paschal Hickman since his intermarriage with his said wife Fanny has had several children, and whereas by the laws of this State the said children follow the condition of their mother.

Sec. 2. Be it therefore enacted by the Senate and House of Representatives of the State of Georgia in General Assembly met, That all said children heretofore born, -- to wit, John, Grove, Henry, William, Hetty, Eliza, and Frank, -- by and in consequence of said intermarriage between the said Paschal Hickman and Fanny his wife, shall be, and they are hereby declared to be free, and placed on the same footing that free persons of colour are usually placed in this State, and entitled to inherit from the said Paschal, as their father, any property which by the laws of this State would go to his children should he die without a will.

Approval Date: Assented to Dec. 22d, 1834.

Acts of the General Assembly of the State of Georgia, passed in Milledgeville, at a Biennial Session, in November, December, January, February & March, 1855-56. Compiled, and notes added, by John W. Duncan.

Part II. Local and Private Laws, Title XXV. Slaves. 1855 Vol. 1, Page: 539. Sequential Number: 537, Law Number: No. 534.

An Act to manumit a negro man slave, named Boston, the property of E. B. Way, Catharine P. Wheeler, Thomas B. Wheeler, H. R. Wheeler, and Eugene Bacon of the State of Georgia, and county of Liberty, and John Savage of the county of Chatham, and State aforesaid.

Whereas, during a long life, the negro man slave, named Boston, has served his owners with uniform fidelity, and whereas, during the war of 1812, he served with his master in the company from Liberty county, which marched to Darien, and remained there under arms in momentary expectation of an engagement with the British who threatened a landing, and other important services to the public.

Sec. I. Be it therefore enacted &c., That in consideration of the services stated in the foregoing preamble, and the petition accompanying this bill, the negro, man slave Boston, the property of E. B Way, Catharine P. Wheeler, Thomas B. Wheeler, H. R. Wheeler, and Eugene Bacon the of county of Liberty, and State aforesaid, and John Savage of the county of Chatham, and State aforesaid, said owners all consenting thereto, be and he is hereby manumitted and forever set free, and shall hereafter enjoy all the rights and privileges to which free negroes in the State of Georgia are entitled.

Approval Date: March 6th, 1856.

Assented to December 22d, 1834.

Acts of the General Assembly of the State of Georgia, passed at Milledgeville, at an Annual Session, in November and December, 1822. Vol. 1, Page: 83. Sequential Number: 080.

An Act to carry into effect the last will and testament of James Robinson late of Greene county, deceased, and to emancipate a female slave by the name of Rachel.

Whereas, the said James Robinson, prior to his death, made a will, containing a clause, among other things, emancipating a female slave by the name of Rachel, the property of him the said James; and whereas the said James, required his executors, to carry this clause of his will into execution, by procuring a legislative act to legalize the same; and the said female slave being desirous of removing to her native state, Maryland:

Sec. 1. Be it therefore enacted by the Senate and House of Representatives of the State of Georgia in General Assembly met, and it is hereby enacted by the authority of the same, That from the passage of this act, the said female slave Rachel, be, and she is hereby fully and completely emancipated and set free according to the intent and meaning of the will of him, the said James Robinson: Provided, that said negro Rachel be, and she is hereby liable to all the fines, penalties and privileges, now imposed and allowed in this state to free people of colour. Provided always that the said Rachel shall not be entitled to the benefits of this act if found in this state within one year after the passing of this act.

14

Acts of the General Assembly of the State of Georgia, passed at Milledgeville, at an Annual Session, in November and December, 1823. Vol. 1, Page: 146. Sequential Number: 113.

An Act to carry into effect the last will and testament of James Robinson, late of Greene county, deceased, so far as to manumit a female slave by the name of Chloe.

Whereas, James Robinson, late of Greene county, deceased, previous to his death, did duly make and publish his last will and testament, containing among other things, a clause emancipating a female slave by the name of Chloe, the property of him the said James -- And whereas, the said James required his executors to carry this clause of his said will into execution, by procuring a legislative act to legalize the same.

Sec. 1. Be it therefore enacted by the Senate and House of Representatives of the State of Georgia, in General Assembly met, and it is hereby enacted by the authority of the same, That from and after the passage of this act, the said female slave Chloe be, and she is hereby fully and completely emancipated and set free, according to the true intent and meaning of him the said James Robinson: Provided, That the said negro Chloe be, and she is hereby liable to all the fines, penalties and privileges, now imposed on, and allowed to, free people of color in this state.

Acts of the General Assembly of the State of Georgia, passed in Milledgeville at an Annual Session in October, November, and December 1830. Vol. 1, Page: 187. Sequential Number: 137.

An Act to emancipate and set free, Joy, Rose and her two sons Jim and John, formerly the property of Ramond Demere, late of St. Simon's Island, in the county of Glynn.

Sec. 1. Be it enacted by the Senate and House of Representatives of the State of Georgia, in General Assembly met, and it is hereby enacted by the authority of the same, That from and after the passage of this act, Joy, Rose and her two sons, Jim and John, formerly the property of Ramond Demere, late of St. Simon's Island, in the county of Glynn, be, and they are hereby emancipated and set free, as an acknowledgment of their extraordinary services in protecting the property of their owner, Ramond Demere of St. Simon's Island, from the depredations of the British Maurauders during the late war with Great Britain: Provided, That the Executors and heirs of the said Demere shall be held liable for the support and maintenance of said slaves, so far as to indemnify the county of Glynn or any other county against all damage by occasion of their infirmity and inability to support themselves.

Sec. 2. And be it further enacted, That the said Joy, Rose and her two sons, Jim and John, be, and they are hereby entitled to all the privileges, and subject to all the laws of this State, for the regulation and Government of free persons of colour.

Approval Date: Assented to December 23d 1830.

Acts of the General Assembly of the State of Georgia, passed in Milledgeville, at an Annual Session in November and December 1834. Vol. 1, Page: 229. Sequential Number: 172.

An Act to emancipate Sam, a negro slave.

Whereas, by a concurred resolution of both branches of the General Assembly of this State, passed at the last session of the Legislature, the Governor of this State, in consideration of the important services rendered by Sam, a negro man slave, in extinguishing the fire on the State-house, was authorized and required to purchase said negro Sam of his owner for the purpose of his emancipation; and his purchase having been effected.

Sec. 1. Be it therefore enacted by the Senate and House of Representatives of the State of Georgia in General Assembly met, and it is hereby enacted by the authority of the same, That from and immediately after the passage of this act, said negro man Sam, formerly the property of John Marler, be, and he is hereby emancipated and set free; and that he enjoy all the privileges and immunities given by the laws of this State to free persons of colour in such manner as if he were born free, -- any law to the contrary notwithstanding.

Approval Date: Assented to 20th December, 1834.

Acts of the General Assembly of the State of Georgia, passed in Milledgeville, at an Annual Session in November and December 1834. Vol. 1 -- Page: 231. Sequential Number: 174.

An Act to emancipate Patsy and Cyrus, the wife and father of Solomon Humphries, a free person of colour; and Edmund, late the property of Theophilus Hill's estate, of Oglethorpe county.

Whereas, Solomon Humphries, a free person of colour, has paid to the former owners of Patsy and Cyrus, his wife and father, the price asked for them.

Sec. 1. Be it therefore enacted by the Senate and House of Representatives of the State of Georgia in General Assembly met, and it is hereby enacted by the authority of the same, That from and immediately after the passing of this act, the said Patsy and Cyrus, the wife and father of Solomon Humphries, and Edmund, late the property of Theophilus Hill's estate, of Oglethorpe county, shall be emancipated and set free, and shall be entitled to all the rights, immunities, and privileges of free persons of colour, as though they had been born free.

Approval Date: Assented to 20th Dec. 1834.

In addition to the manumissions, the legislature enacted laws concerning three separate free persons of color.

Acts of the General Assembly of the State of Georgia: Passed at Milledgeville, at an Extra Session, in April and May, 1821. Volume I – Page: 20. Sequential Number: 109.

An Act for the relief of Austin, otherwise called Austin Dabney, a Freeman of colour.

Whereas, by an act of the General Assembly of the state of Georgia, passed on the fourteenth day of August, 1786, it is stated that the said Austin, during the Revolution, instead of advantaging himself of the times to withdraw from the American lines and enter with the majority of his color and fellow-slaves in the service of his Britannic Majesty, and his officers and vassals, did voluntarily enroll himself in some one of the corps under the command of Col. Elijah Clark, and in several actions and engagements behaved against the common enemy with a bravery and fortitude which would have honored a freeman; and in one of which engagements he was severely wounded and rendered incapable of hard servitude; and policy as well as gratitude, demand a return for such services and behavior from the Commonwealth; and it was further stated in said act, that said Austin "should be entitled to the annuity allowed by this state, to wounded and disabled soldiers." And the said Austin having petitioned the Legislature for some aid in his declining years, and this body considering him an object entitled to the attention and gratitude of the state he has defended, and in whose service he has been disabled;

Sec. 1. Be it enacted by the Senate and House of Representatives in General Assembly met, and it is hereby enacted by the same, That the lot or fraction of land situate, lying and being in the county of Walton, in the first district, and known and distinguished by number two hundred and eighty four, containing one hundred and twelve acres, be the same more or less, be and the same hereby is conveyed and transferred to the said Austin during the period of the natural life of him the said Austin Dabney.

Sec. 2. And be it further enacted, That the Austin Dabney be, and is hereby entitled to a plat for the same.

Sec. 3. And be it further enacted, That the lot and number above named is, and shall be exempted from the contemplated sale of Fractions in said county, authorized by an act at the annual session of the Legislature, in the year 1820.

Assented to, 16th May, 1821.

Acts of the General Assembly of the State of Georgia: Passed in Milledgeville, at a Biennial Session, in November, December, January, February & March, 1855-56. Compiled, and Notes Added, by John W. Duncan. Part II – Local and Private Laws. Title XXV. Slaves. 1855. Volume I – Page: 539. Sequential Number: 536. Law Number: 533.

An Act to exempt Daniel and Lucinda his wife, the property of Harrison W. Riley, nominal slaves from the tax now imposed by law on nominal slaves.

3. Sec. 1. Be it enacted, &c., That Daniel, the property of Harrison W. Riley, and Lucinda, the wife of said Daniel, nominal slaves, be exempt from the tax now imposed by law on nominal slaves, and that they be required to pay only such tax as now required by law from free persons of color.

Approved, March 5th, 1856.

Acts of the General Assembly of the State of Georgia: Passed in Milledgeville, at an Annual Session, in November and December, 1862. Title IX. Slaves and Free Persons of Color. Volume I. Sequential Number: 101.

An Act to authorize Jane Miller, a free person of color, to sell herself into perpetual slavery.

1. Sec. 1. Be it enacted &c., That Jane Miller, a free person of color, in Clarke county be, and she is hereby authorized to voluntarily become the slave of E. S. Sims for life.

2. Sec. II. That in order to carry into effect the first section of this Act, the said E. S. Sims and the said Jane Miller, shall go before the Justices of the Inferior Court, or a majority of them, in said county, who shall faithfully and fully examine her as to her willingness to become the slave for life of said E. S. Sone; and upon being satisfied of the same, they shall pass an order to the effect that the said Jane Miller be held, deemed and considered he slave of the said E. S. Sims for and during her natural life, subject to all the incidents of slavery, except the liability of being sold during the lifetime of said Sims, by himself, or his creditors for his debts; he sole consideration for which voluntary enslavement on her part, shall be the obligation thereby incurred by her master of feeding, clothing and protecting her.

3. Sec III. It shall be the duty of the Clerk of the Inferior Court to record said order on the minutes of the Court as evidence of title; also to record the same in the book kept by him for recording other evidences of title to property; for which the said E. S. Sims shall pay to said Clerk a fee of five dollars.

Assented to December 9th, 1862.

18

First Register, 1812

The following is a transcription from the original record volume. On the cover the clerk wrote

A list of Free persons of Color, returned under the Act of 15th December 1810.

On top of the first page, the clerk wrote

A list of persons of colour returned to the Clerk of the Superior Court of Richmond County under the "Act for regulating and governing free persons of color coming into the State or residing therein." Passed 15th December 1810.

The register contains only two entries.

James Triplet, by W. Barton, Guardian, occupation laborer, born Virginia, came to Georgia to reside, employed by Cha⁸ Labuzan upon arrival, last from Virginia, amount received $20.00, when received 23 May 1812, to whom paid by the clerk Jno. D'Autiguat, T. C., when returned 23 May 1812

Dan¹ Caroline, by J. Jones, Guardian, occupation carpenter, born North Carolina, came to Georgia to reside, employed by no person upon arrival, last from North Carolina, amount received $20.00, when received 23 May 1812, to whom paid by the clerk Superior Court order, when returned 23 May 1812

Second Register, 1819-1847

On the inside Cover of the original record volume, a clerk wrote

Richmond County
Registration of Free
Persons of Color
under Act of 1818
1819-1847

[Inferior Court Records
Office of Ordinary]

On a separate slip of paper, the clerk affixed the following certificate to the first page

Georgia　　}
Richm^d Ct^y　} Clerk's Office, Inferior Court

I Certify that the following is a correct list of the names of persons of color registered in this office, in conformity to the Act of the 19th December 1818, Supplementary to and now effectually to enforce an act prescribing the mode of manumitting slaves in this State, &c and all persons concerned or interested will take notice that Certificates will issue to them, on or before the first Monday in May, if objecting and not filed thereto, on or before the second Monday in April next, to wit

On the next page, the clerk wrote

Record of the names, ages, places of nativity, and residence time of coming into Georgia, and occupation or pursuit of free persons of color in the County of Richmond, under the Act of the General Assembly of this State passed the 19th December 1818, Supplementary to and more effectually to enforce an act entitled an Act prescribing the mode of manumitting Slaves in this State, to prevent the future migration of free persons of color thereto; to regulate Such free persons of color, as now reside therein, and for other purposes.

The original volume is not page numbered. In addition to the occupation or pursuit listed in the last column, the clerk noted either "Grant a Certificate" or "No Certificate." The following transcription notes only when no certificate was issued.

The following transcription consists of a series of tables usually providing the name of the registrant, their age, place of nativity, when they came to Georgia, their occupation, and residence, and sometimes providing the name of their guardian, and each table usually covering one year of registrations.

Returns for 1819

Name	Age	Nativity	Residence	How Long in Georgia	Occupation
Charles Grant	50	North Carolina	Augusta	20 years ago	Carpenter
Peter Johnson, dead	46	Savannah	Augusta		Carpenter
Sally Johnson	16	Augusta	Augusta		Seamstress
John Johnson, dead	14	Augusta	Augusta		Carpenter
Caty Johnson	7	Augusta	Augusta		No occupation
Billy Johnson, dead	11	Augusta	Augusta		No occupation
Peter Johnson, Junr	9	Augusta	Augusta		No occupation
Nancy Johnson	3	Augusta	Augusta		No occupation
Nancy Johnson	43	South Carolina	Augusta		Washing
Nancy Fox	55	Augusta	Augusta		Washing No Certificate
Junno Kelly	20	Augusta	Augusta		Seamstress
Betsey Kelly	22	Augusta	Augusta		Washing
George Kelly	19	Augusta	Augusta		Carpenter
Alfred Kelly	3 mos	Augusta	Augusta		
Sam Kelly	5	Augusta	Augusta		
Richd Kelly, dead	70	South Carolina	Augusta	25 years ago	Common laborer
Josiah Kelly	1	Georgia	Augusta		

Name	Age	Nativity	Residence	How Long in Georgia	Occupation
Venus Maher	55	Guinea	Augusta	30 years ago	Washing
Vienna Kelly, dead	22	Augusta	Augusta		Seamstress
Henry Kelly	2	Augusta	Augusta		
Sally Langley	35	Maryland	Augusta	22 years ago	Washing No Certificate
Isabella Willson	20	Georgia	Augusta		Seamstress
Sarah Carns, dead	35	North Carolina	Augusta	8 years ago	Seamstress
Jack Carns, dead	22	South Carolina	Augusta	15 years ago	Boating
Joe Carns	20	South Carolina	Augusta	15 years ago	Boating
Vienna Carns	15	South Carolina	Augusta	14 years ago	Seamstress
Lucy Carns	20	South Carolina	Augusta	15 years ago	Seamstress
Thomas Carter	26	Maryland	Augusta	14 years ago	Carpenter
Sarah Richards	30	South Carolina	Augusta	20 years ago	Seamstress
Junno Course	30	Augusta	Augusta		Seamstress
Mariah Monroe, or Page	18	Augusta	Augusta		Seamstress postponed as before
Edy Sheftall	26	Savannah	Augusta	25	Seamstress No appearance No Certificate
Charlotte Tubman	20	Augusta	Augusta		Seamstress No Certificate

22

Name	Age	Nativity	Residence	How Long in Georgia	Occupation
Sarah Walton	25	Augusta	Augusta		Washing No Certificate
Chloe Walton	50	Savannah	Augusta		Washing No ~~answer~~ No Certificate
Martha Walton	5	Augusta	Augusta		No Certificate
Betsey Magnan	40	St Domingo	Augusta	25 years	Washing No ~~answer~~ No Certificate
James Triplet	60	Virginia	Augusta	10 years	Waggoning
Maryann Triplet	19	Virginia	Augusta	2 years Slave	Washing, cooking, &c
Richard Triplet	13	Virginia	Augusta	10 years	Waggoning &c No Certificate
James Triplet, Junr	2	Augusta	Augusta		No Certificate
Sambo Campbell	70	South Carolina	Augusta (not free)	60	Gardening No Certificate, because his is claimed
Thomas Kelly	25	South Carolina	Augusta	20 years	Boating
Mary Jenne Cloe	32	St Domingo	Augusta	25 years	Washing ~~no answer~~
Jenney Ross	60	Georgia	Augusta		Washing &c
Thomas Bradley	79	Virginia	Richmond County	8 months	carpenter
Amelia Brown	23	Virginia	Augusta	15 years	Sewing
Ellener Knight	30	South Carolina	Augusta	7 years	Sewing

23

Name	Age	Nativity	Residence	How Long in Georgia	Occupation
Benjamin Knight	2	Savannah	Augusta		
Peggy Haynes	24	Columbia County	Augusta		House servant
Bob Martin	23	Richmond County	Augusta		Draying
Nelly Kelly	23	Augusta	Augusta	23 years	Washing
John Kelly	9	Augusta	Augusta	9 years	
Jane Scott	17	Augusta	Augusta	17 years	Seamstress
Elenor Harris	29	Edgefield District	Augusta	12	Seamstress
Robert Kelly	12	South Carolina	Augusta	1 year	House servant
Gilbert Madison Scott	7	South Carolina	Augusta	3 years	
James Larry	51	Virginia	Augusta	30 years	Laborer
Katey Larry	20	Augusta	Augusta		Weaver No Certificate
Eliza Larry	10	Augusta	Augusta		No occupation
James Larry, Jun[r]	8	Augusta	Augusta		No occupation
Nelly Jones	30	Virginia	Augusta	16 years	Washing
Robert Jones	14	Augusta	Augusta	14 years	Bound to the H. Penn
Saphelia Jones	7	Augusta	Augusta	7 years	
Mary Ann Jones	1	Augusta	Augusta	1 year	

Name	Age	Nativity	Residence	How Long in Georgia	Occupation
Augustus Lary	1	Augusta	Augusta	1 year	No Certificate
Daniel Caroline	35	North Carolina	Augusta	8 years	Carpenter
Rachael Chavers	30	South Carolina	Augusta	22 years	Washing & sewing
Linda Lambert	50	South Carolina	Augusta	22 years	Marketing
Suckey Young	50	Virginia	Augusta	15 years	Washing No Certificate
Nancy Kevan	27	Georgia	Augusta	27 years	Washing
Urselle Poisson	21	North Carolina	Augusta	18 years	Sewing
Betsey Keating	27	South Carolina	Augusta	26 years	Sewing
Caroline Keating	9	Georgia	Augusta	9 years	Sewing
Emily Keating	7	Georgia	Augusta	7 years	
Eliz[a] Keating	5	Georgia	Augusta	5 years	
Joseph Keating	3	Georgia	Augusta	3 years	
Casar Tanner	76	South Carolina	Springfield	2 years	Sexton to the African church
Sophia	78	South Carolina	Springfield	25 years	25
Maryland		South Carolina	Augusta	9 years	Weavering
Billy Collins	55	South Carolina	Augusta	25 years	Boating No Certificate
Roderick Dent	25	Maryland	Augusta	15 years	Blacksmith postponed as

Name	Age	Nativity	Residence	How Long in Georgia	Occupation
					before
Kittey Shefton	13	Augusta	Augusta		Seamstress No Certificate
Lewis Monroe	4 mos	Augusta	Augusta	4 months	No occupation postponed as before
Williss Carter	26	Virginia	Augusta	22 years	Carpenter
Joseph Smith	22	Augusta	Augusta		Sadling No Certificate bound to Capt McKinn
James Lee	16	Savannah	Augusta	5 years	Farmer
David Russell	13	Barnwell, South Carolina	Augusta	2 years	Farmer
John Wright	30	Georgia	Richmond County		Planter
Polly Wright	32	Georgia	Richmond County		Spinning, weaving, &c
Juda Coleman	14	South Carolina	Richmond County	11 months	Spinning & weaving No answer No Certificate
Moses Jones	65		Augusta	20 years	Boat hand
Jacob T. Welsh	27	New Ark	Augusta	4 months	Harness maker & trimmer
Isaac Harman	27	Georgia	Richmond County	27 years	Common laborer
Mathew Harman	25	Georgia	Richmond County	25 years	Common laborer

Name	Age	Nativity	Residence	How Long in Georgia	Occupation
James Harman	22	Georgia	Richmond County	22 years	Common laborer
Abraham Harman	20	Georgia	Richmond County	20 years	Common laborer
Alcey Ragland	50	Virginia	Augusta	32 years	Spinning, Sewing, &c No Certificate
Martha Hewlen	36	South Carolina	Richmond County	12 years	Spinning & sewing
John Evans	54	Virginia	Richmond County	35 years	Millwright
James Evans	9	Richmond County	Richmond County		No occupation
William Hulen	14	South Carolina	Richmond County	12 years	Farming
Sarah Hulen	13	Richmond County	Richmond County		
Mary Hulen	12	Richmond County	Richmond County	12 years	Washing
Mavel Hulen	9	Richmond County	Richmond County	9 years	House work
John Hulen	7	Richmond County	Richmond County	7 years	No occupation
Anny Hulen	5	Richmond County	Richmond County	5 years	No occupation
Betsey Bond, or Mullin	25	South Carolina	Augusta	24 years	Washing
John Cousins	55	Virginia	Richmond County	5 years	Ostler
Priscilla Bing	43	South	Richmond	23 years	Spinning &

Name	Age	Nativity	Residence	How Long in Georgia	Occupation
		Carolina	County		weaving
Salley Rouse	22	Georgia	Richmond County	22 years	Spinning, weaving, & sewing
William Evans	20	Georgia	Richmond County	20 years	Common laborer
Nero Freeman	23	Connecticut	Augusta	3 years	Barber & waitenman ~~withdrawn by consent~~
Aron Keating	30	South Carolina	Augusta	28 years	Waiter subject to investigation, referred as before
Ned Harris					
Bettey Willson	50				
~~Henry Williams~~	~~27~~	~~Pennsylvania~~	~~Augusta~~	~~5 years~~	~~Common laborer~~

Returns for 1820

The following list is not dated, but is separated from the previous list by a blank page. Based upon the repeated names one year older than they appear on the previous list, the following list apparently is for the year 1820.

The list does not indicate whether or not a certificate was issued.

Name	Age	Nativity	Residence	How long in Georgia	Occupation
William Hill	43	Virginia	Augusta	26 years	Barber
Jenny Keating	36	Virginia	Augusta	25 years	Washing
Polly Keating	13	Augusta	Augusta	From her birth	Seamstress
Betsey Keating	12	Augusta	Augusta	From her birth	Seamstress
Th° Keating	4	Augusta	Augusta	From his birth	
Aug⁵ Keating	1½	Augusta	Augusta	From his birth	
Henry Willson	27	Pennsylvania	Augusta	5 years	Common laborer
Moses Hill	46	Maryland	Augusta	40 years	Boatman
Mason Harris	56	North Carolina	Augusta	40 years	Rafting
Bob Martin	23	Augusta	Augusta	From his birth	Boat hand
Moses Jones	60	South Carolina	Augusta	42 years	Boat hand
Stephen Frost	64	Baltimore	Augusta	20 years	Boat caulker
Tom Paris	50	Richmond County	Augusta	From birth	Boat hand
Patsey Hill	40	Chatham	Augusta		Seamstress

Name	Age	Nativity	Residence	How long in Georgia	Occupation
		County			
Charles Grant	50	Virginia	Augusta	30 years	Carpenter
Jack Harris	53	Maryland	Augusta	Upwards of 41 years	Boating
Rachel Harris	14	Savannah	Augusta		House servant
Aluk Pope	38	Maryland	Augusta	20 years	Drayman
Judy Kelly	30	South Carolina	Augusta	22 years	Cake baker & sausage maker
Thomas Carter	27	Maryland	Augusta	13 years	Carpenter
William Kelly	14	Augusta	Augusta	Since his birth	Carpenter
Madison Kelly	11	Augusta	Augusta	Since his birth	No occupation
Augustus Kelly	10	Augusta	Augusta	Since his birth	No occupation
Ann Kelly	6	Augusta	Augusta	Since her birth	No occupation
Emily Kelly	4	Augusta	Augusta	Since her birth	No occupation
Nelly Kelly	20	Augusta	Augusta	Since her birth	Seamstress
James Triplett	63	Virginia	Augusta	11 years	Wagoner
Linda Lambert	51	South Carolina	Augusta	23 years	Marketing
Peter Johnson	46	Savannah	Augusta		Carpenter
Sally Johnson	16	Augusta	Augusta		Seamstress
John Johnson	14	Augusta	Augusta		Carpenter

Name	Age	Nativity	Residence	How long in Georgia	Occupation
Catey Johnson	7	Augusta	Augusta		No occupation
Betty Johnson	11	Augusta	Augusta		No occupation
Peter Johnson, Junr	9	Augusta	Augusta		No occupation
Nancy Johnson	43	South Carolina	Augusta		No occupation
Jane Scott	18	Augusta	Augusta		Seamstress & washer
Venus Maher	56	Guine	Augusta	31 years ago	Seamstress
Margarett Haynes	19	Richmond County	Augusta		Washing, cooking, &c
Willis Carter	26	Virginia	Augusta	20	Carpenter
Harriet Williams	37	South Carolina	Augusta	10	Seamstress
Nelly Jones	31	Virginia	Augusta	16	Washing
Robert Jones	15	Augusta	Augusta		Bound to T. H. Penn
Sofelia Jones	8	Augusta	Augusta		
Mary Ann Jones	2	Augusta	Augusta		
Aron Keating	30	South Carolina	Augusta	22	Boot cleaner
Sarah Rouse, or Keating	37	South Carolina	Augusta	21	Washing & seamstress
Ursula Stith	22	North Carolina	Augusta	14	No occupation
Vienna Kelly	25	Augusta	Augusta	25	Seamstress
Sarah Carnes	36	North	Augusta	9	Seamstress

Name	Age	Nativity	Residence	How long in Georgia	Occupation
		Carolina			
Lucy Carnes	21	South Carolina	Augusta	16	Seamstress
Wm Carnes	1 mo	Georgia	Augusta		
Vienna Carnes	16	South Carolina	Augusta	16	Seamstress
Betsey Keating	28	South Carolina	Augusta	27	Seamstress
Caroline Keating	10	South Carolina	Augusta	9	Seamstress
Emily Keating	8	Augusta	Augusta	8	Seamstress
Eliza Keating	6	Augusta	Augusta	6	Seamstress
Joseph Keating	4	Augusta	Augusta	4	
Vilet Harper	65	Maryland	Augusta	30	Washing & cooking
Isabella Willson	21	Columbia County	Augusta	21	Seamstress
Mariah Munroe	19	Augusta	Augusta	19	Seamstress
Nancy Fox		Augusta	Augusta		Sausage maker

Second Returns for 1820

Across the top of the page, the clerk wrote

Entered on and since the first day of March 1820

Name	Age	Nativity	Residence	How long in Georgia	Occupation
Nanny Harris	63	Virginia	Augusta	30 years	Washing
Jacob Wright	32	Georgia	Richmond County	From his birth	Common laborer
Polly Wright	30	Georgia	Richmond County	From her birth	Common housework
Jack Carnes	22	South Carolina	Augusta	15 years	Boating
Joe Carnes	21	South Carolina	Augusta	15 years	Boating
John Cousins	56	Virginia	Richmond County	6 years	Ostler
Cloe Bignan	32	St Domingo	Augusta	22 years	Washing, Serving, &c.
John Evans	55	Virginia	Richmond County	35 years	Millwright
Prisse Evans	45	South Carolina	Richmond County	24 years	Common housework
James Evans	11	Georgia	Richmond County		
William Evans	22	Georgia	Richmond County		Common laborer
Sally Brunson	20	South Carolina	Richmond County	19	Common laborer
John Brunson	7 mos	Georgia	Richmond County		

33

Name	Age	Nativity	Residence	How long in Georgia	Occupation
Daniel Caroline	35	North Carolina	Augusta	9	Carpenter
Marheed Caroline	6	Augusta	Augusta		

Returns for 1821

The following list is not dated, but is separated from the previous list by a blank page. Based upon the repeated names one year older than they appear on the previous list, the following list apparently is for the year 1821.

Name	Age	Nativity	Residence	How long in Georgia	Occupation
James Triplet	64	Virginia	Augusta	12 years	Wagoner
Richard Triplet	15	Virginia	Augusta	11 years	Wagoning
Mariah Triplet	2	Augusta	Augusta		
Sarah Carnes	37	South Carolina	Augusta	10	Seamstress
Lucy Carnes	22	South Carolina	Augusta	16	Seamstress
James Carnes	1	Georgia	Augusta		
Vienna Carnes	17	Georgia	Augusta		Seamstress
Jack Carnes	23	South Carolina	Augusta	15 years	Boating
Joe Carnes	22	South Carolina	Augusta	15 years	Boating
Rachael Chavers	30	South Carolina	Augusta	22 years	Washing & sewing
Edmund Chavers	2	Georgia	Augusta		
Vilet Harper	66	Maryland	Augusta	30	Washer &c
Betsey Keating	29	South Carolina	Augusta	28 years	Sewing
Caroline Keating	11	Georgia	Augusta		Sewing
Emily Keating	9	Georgia	Augusta		Sewing
Elizabeth	7	Georgia	Augusta		Sewing

Name	Age	Nativity	Residence	How long in Georgia	Occupation
Keating					
Joseph Keating	5	Georgia	Augusta		Sewing
Lear Larry	27	Georgia	Augusta		Seamstress
Katey Larry	23	Georgia	Augusta		Weaver
Vienna Kelly	24	Georgia	Augusta		Sewing & washing
Henry Kelly	3	Georgia	Augusta		
Sarah Fitz	35	South Carolina	Augusta	30 years	Washing & sewing
Andrew Fitz	2	Augusta	Augusta		
Likey Fitz	7	Augusta	Augusta		
Mariah Monroe	20	Augusta	Augusta		Seamstress
Amey Dobins	27	Augusta	Augusta		Washing & ironing
Silvester Dobins	7	Augusta	Augusta		
Edneyborough Dobins	5	Augusta	Augusta		
Betsey Kelly	23	Augusta	Augusta		Washer
Samuel Kelly	6	Augusta	Augusta		
Josiah Kelly	3	Augusta	Augusta		
Margarett Kelly	1	Augusta	Augusta		
Deborah Kelly	40	South Carolina	Augusta	23	Washing &c
Jenny Keating	37	Virginia	Augusta	26	Washing
Polly Keating	14	Augusta	Augusta	From birth	Seamstress

Name	Age	Nativity	Residence	How long in Georgia	Occupation
Betsey Keating	13	Augusta	Augusta	From birth	
Thos Keating	5	Augusta	Augusta	From birth	
Augustus Keating	2½	Augusta	Augusta	From birth	
Nelly Kelly	27	Augusta	Augusta	27 years	Seamstress
John Kelly	11	Augusta	Augusta	11 years	House boy
Jency Scott	18	Augusta	Augusta	18 years	seamstress
Nancy Harris	64	Virginia	Augusta	31 years	Washing
Anna Kelly	30	Augusta	Richmond County	30 years	Washing
Sally Johnson	21	Augusta	Augusta	From birth	Washing
Wm Johnson	4	Augusta	Augusta	From birth	
James Johnson	2	Augusta	Augusta	From birth	
Lunday Lambert	52	South Carolina	Augusta	2 years	marketing
Nancy Fox	56	Augusta	Augusta	Birth	Sausage maker
Sarah Ross	33	South Carolina	Augusta	22	Seamstress
Tom Paris	51	Richmond County	Augusta	From birth	Boating
Milley Sibble	40	Maryland	Augusta	20	Washing
John G. Evans	56	Virginia	Richmond County	37	Millwright
James Evans	11	Georgia	Richmond County	From birth	
Pricilla Evans	45	South	Richmond	23	Seamstress

Name	Age	Nativity	Residence	How long in Georgia	Occupation
		Carolina	County		
John Rouse	51	North Carolina	Richmond County	15 years	Sawyer
Vicey Rouse	38	South Carolina	Richmond County	15	Seamstress
Irena Rouse	6	Georgia	Richmond County	From birth	
Henry Rouse	3	Georgia	Richmond County	From birth	
Gilbert Scott	9	Georgia	Richmond County	From birth	
John Foster	34	Charles City County, Virginia	Augusta	7 months	Waiting man, Thomas Pace & Nat Clarke, Guardian

Returns for 1822

Name	Age	Nativity	Residence	How long in Georgia	Occupation
Myra Dent	21	Columbia, Georgia	Augusta	From birth	Seamstress
Bob Martin	26	Augusta	Augusta	From birth	February 1822
Harriet Williams	30	Beach Island	Augusta	12 years	Seamstress, weaver, & washer
William Hill	43	Virginia	Augusta	35 years	Barber
Patsy Hill, his wife	40	Georgia	Augusta	35 years	Seamstress
Lewis Brux	9	Georgia	Augusta	9 years	
Sarah Carnes	38	South Carolina	Augusta	20 years	Seamstress
Vienna Carnes	28	South Carolina	Augusta	16 years	Seamstress
Lucy Carnes	23	South Carolina	Augusta	17	Seamstress
James Carnes	2	Augusta	Augusta	2	
Vienna Kelly	25	Augusta	Augusta	25	Seamstress
Henry Kelly	4	Augusta	Augusta	4	Seamstress
Nancy Fox	57	Augusta	Augusta	From birth	Sausage maker
Tom Parris	52	Augusta	Augusta	From Birth	Boating
Lear Hawkins	40	Savannah	Augusta	From birth	Seamstress & washer
Tom Carter	28	Maryland	Augusta	11 years	Carpenter & waiter
Aaron Keating	34	South	Augusta	24 years	Drayman

Name	Age	Nativity	Residence	How long in Georgia	Occupation
		Carolina			
Sarah Keating, or Rouse	39	South Carolina	Augusta	23 years	Washer & seamstress
Violet Harper	70	Maryland	Augusta	30 years	Washer &c
Betsy Keating	30	South Carolina	Augusta	29 years	Seamstress
Caroline Keating	12	Georgia	Augusta	12	Sewing
Emily Keating	10	Augusta	Augusta	10	Sewing
Elizabeth Keating	7	Augusta	Augusta	7	Sewing
John Keating	3	Augusta	Augusta	3	
Eleanor Harris	29	South Carolina	Augusta	28	Seamstress
Gilbert Scot	10	Georgia	Augusta	10	
Jinny Keating	38	Virginia	Augusta	30	Washer & seamstress
Polly Keating	15	Augusta	Augusta	15	
Betsy Keating	14	Augusta	Augusta	14	
Thos Keating	6	Augusta	Augusta	6	
Augustus Keating	3½	Augusta	Augusta	3½	
Maria Monroe	21	Augusta	Augusta	21	Seamstress
Louis Monroe	3	Augusta	Augusta	3	
Mary Monroe	2	Augusta	Augusta	2	
John Monroe	6 mos	Augusta	Augusta	6 months	

Name	Age	Nativity	Residence	How long in Georgia	Occupation
Jim Triplett	69	Virginia	Augusta	13 years	Wagoner
Richard Triplett	16	Virginia	Augusta	12 years	Wagoner
Maria Triplett	3	Virginia	Augusta	3	
Alleck Pope	40	Pennsylvania	Augusta	23 years	Drayman
Venice Mahar	57	Africa	Augusta	40 years	Washer
Sally Ross	34	South Carolina	Augusta	23 years	Seamstress
Lear Larrie	28	Georgia	Augusta	28 years	seamstress
Katy Larrie	24	Georgia	Augusta	24 years	Seamstress
Shadrack Cadey	30	Virginia	Augusta	10 years	Boatman
Isabella Lamar	23	Georgia	Augusta	23 years	Seamstress
Betsy McFarlane	40	Virginia	Augusta	36 years	Weaving & washer
Jack Carnes	23	Georgia	Augusta	23 years	Boatman
Joe Carnes	21	Georgia	Augusta	21 years	Boatman
Judy Kelly	37	South Carolina	Augusta	30 years	Seamstress
William Kelly	14	Georgia	Augusta	14	Apprentice to the blacksmith
Madison Kelly	12	Georgia	Augusta	12	
Augustus Kelly	10	Georgia	Augusta	10	
Ann Kelly	7	Georgia	Augusta	7	
Emily Kelly	5	Georgia	Augusta	5	
Samuel Kelly	3 mos	Georgia	Augusta	3	

Name	Age	Nativity	Residence	How long in Georgia	Occupation
Nelly Kelly	29	Georgia	Augusta	29	Seamstress
John Kelly	8 11	Georgia	Augusta	8	
Jane Scott	28	Georgia	Augusta	28	Seamstress
Rachael Chavers	45	South Carolina	Augusta	23	Washer
Edmund Chavers	3	Georgia	Augusta	3	
Betsy Kelly	24	Georgia	Augusta	23	Washer & seamstress
Samuel Kelly	7	Georgia	Augusta	6	
Josiah Kelly	3	Georgia	Augusta	3	
Margaret Kelly	2	Georgia	Augusta	2	
Charles Grant	51	Virginia	Augusta	36	Carpenter
Deborah Kelly	40	South Carolina	Augusta	24	Washer & seamstress
Cloe Bignon	32	St Domingo	Augusta	24	Washer & seamstress
Sally Johnson	22	Augusta	Augusta	22	Washer & seamstress
James Johnson	2	Augusta	Augusta	2	Washer & seamstress
William Johnson	3	Augusta	Augusta	3	Washer & seamstress
Ann Kelly	33	South Carolina	Augusta	30	Washer & seamstress
Nanny Harris	60	South Carolina	Augusta	40	Washer

Name	Age	Nativity	Residence	How long in Georgia	Occupation
Patsey Lett	28	North Carolina	Augusta	20	Washer
Willis Lett	12	Georgia	Augusta	12	
Martha Commander	20	South Carolina	Augusta	5 years	seamstress
Mary Commander	24	South Carolina	Augusta	5 years	seamstress
Eliza Commander	10	South Carolina	Augusta	5 years	seamstress
Matild Commander	50	South Carolina	Augusta	5 years	seamstress
Susan Commander	16	South Carolina	Augusta	5 years	seamstress
Judy Commander	12	South Carolina	Augusta	5 years	
George Campbell	21	South Carolina	Augusta	21 years	Boat hand
Roderick Dent	28	Maryland	Augusta	11 years	Waiter
Cloe Dent	26	Maryland	Augusta	11	Seamstress
Jacob Dent	30	Maryland	Augusta	11 years	Carpenter
Myra Dent	18	Maryland	Augusta	11 years	Seamstress
Stephen Frost	69	Maryland	Augusta	35 years	Caulker
Lindy Lambert	57	South Carolina	Augusta	40 years	Washer
Elizabeth Esterling	48	St Domingo	Augusta	30 years	Seamstress
Elizabeth Esterling	27	Georgia	Augusta	27 years	Seamstress

Name	Age	Nativity	Residence	How long in Georgia	Occupation
Mason Harris	60	North Carolina	Augusta	50	Wagoner
Lewis Carter	36	District Columbia	Augusta	23	Carter
Milly Sibley	45	Maryland	Augusta	20	Washer & ironer
Amy Dobbins	28	South Carolina	Augusta	8	Washer & ironer
David Knight	23	Georgia	Augusta	23	Boatman, entered this 19th Decr 1822, stating sickness prevented his coming sooner

Returns for 1823

Name	Age	Nativity	Residence	How long in Georgia	Occupation
Isaac Harman	30	Georgia	Augusta	30	Farmer
Sarah Carnes	39	South Carolina	Augusta	21	Seamstress
Vienna Carnes	16	South Carolina	Augusta	15	Seamstress
Jack Carnes	23	South Carolina	Augusta	20	Boatman
Lucy Carnes	21	South Carolina	Augusta	20	Seamstress
James Carnes	2	Georgia	Augusta	2	
Mary Ann Carnes, dead	1	Georgia	Augusta	1	
Sally Ross	35	South Carolina	Augusta	34	Seamstress
Patsey Commander	22	South Carolina	Augusta	7	Seamstress
Susan Commander	19	South Carolina	Augusta	7	Seamstress
Matilda Commander	50	South Carolina	Augusta	7	Seamstress
Mary Commander	24	South Carolina	Augusta	7	Seamstress
Eliza Commander	11	South Carolina	Augusta	7	Seamstress
Sarah Johnson	21	Georgia	Augusta	21 years	Seamstress
William Johnson	5	Georgia	Augusta	5	
James Johnson	4	Georgia	Augusta	4	

Name	Age	Nativity	Residence	How long in Georgia	Occupation
Mathew Harman	28	Georgia	Richmond County	28	Laborer
Tom Carter	29	Maryland	Augusta	12	Carpenter
Shadrack Casey	31	Virginia	Augusta	11	Boatman
William Hill	44	Virginia	Augusta	36	Barber
Patsey Hill, his wife	40	Georgia	Augusta	36	Seamstress
Lewis Brux	10	Georgia	Augusta	10	Apprentice to barber
Judy Kelly	38	South Carolina	Augusta	31	Seamstress
William Kelly	15	Georgia	Augusta	15	Apprentice to blacksmith
Madison Kelly	13	Georgia	Augusta	13	
Augustus Kelly	11	Georgia	Augusta		
Ann Kelly	8	Georgia	Augusta		
Emily Kelly	6	Georgia	Augusta		
Bob Martin	27	Augusta	Augusta	27	Laborer
Harriet Williams	31	South Carolina	Augusta	12	Seamstress & weaver
Viella Kelly	26	Augusta	Augusta	26	Seamstress & washer
Joe Carnes	22	Georgia	Augusta	22	Boatman
Isabella Lamar	24	Georgia	Augusta	24	Seamstress
Moses Sparrow	27	Norfolk, Virginia	Augusta	18	Carpenter

Name	Age	Nativity	Residence	How long in Georgia	Occupation
Mason Harris	61	North Carolina	Augusta	27	Wagoner
Tom Parris	55	Georgia	Augusta	55	Boatman
John Hilton	27	Virginia	Augusta	2	Printer
Katy Larry	23	Georgia	Augusta	23	Seamstress
Venice Mahan	58	Africa	Augusta	41	Washer
Polly Keating	16	Augusta	Augusta	16	Seamstress
Betsey Keating	15	Augusta	Augusta	15	Seamstress
Augustus Keating	4	Augusta	Augusta	4	
Thomas Keating	8	Augusta	Augusta	8	
Jenny Keating	39	Virginia	Augusta	30	
Robert Keating	8 mos	Augusta	Augusta	8	
Maria Triplett	4	Augusta	Augusta	4	Wagoner
Jim Triplett	70	Virginia	Augusta	13	Wagoner
Richd Triplett	17	Virginia	Augusta	13	Wagoner
Jacob Dent	32	Maryland	Augusta	12 years	Carpenter
Cloe Dent	26	Maryland	Augusta	12 years	Seamstress
Laura Dent	18	Maryland	Augusta	1 year	Seamstress
Roderick Dent	29	Maryland	Augusta	12 years	Coachman
Alec Pope	41	Pennsylvania	Augusta	24 years	Drayman
Nancy Fox	58	Augusta	Augusta	From birth	Sausage maker
Betsey Kelly	26	Augusta	Augusta	21	Anything

Name	Age	Nativity	Residence	How long in Georgia	Occupation
Samuel Kelly	7	Augusta	Augusta	7	Child
Josiah Kelly	6	Augusta	Augusta	6	Child
Margaret Kelly	3	Augusta	Augusta	5	Child
Harrington Kelly	1	Augusta	Augusta	1	Child
George Kelly	19	Augusta	Augusta	19	Painter

Returns for 1824

The table has no column headings, but appears to contain the same information as in previous years.

Name	Age	Nativity	Residence	How long in Georgia	Occupation
Bob Martin	28	Augusta	Augusta	28 years	Laborer
Harriet Williams	37	South Carolina	Augusta	12 years	Seamstress & weaver
Tom Parris	56	Georgia	Augusta	56	Boatman
Sarah Carnes	40	South Carolina	Augusta	22	Seamstress
Viana Carnes	16	Georgia	Augusta	16	Seamstress
Judy Kelly	39	South Carolina	Augusta	32	Seamstress
William Kelly	16	Georgia	Augusta	16	
Madison Kelly	14	Georgia	Augusta	14	
Augustus Kelly	12	Georgia	Augusta	12	
Ann Kelly	9	Georgia	Augusta	9	
Emily Kelly	7	Georgia	Augusta	7	
Lucy Carnes	22	Georgia	Augusta	22	Seamstress
James Carnes	3	Georgia	Augusta	3	
Tom Carter	30	Maryland	Augusta	13	Carpenter & waiter
Nancy Fox	59	Augusta	Augusta	59	Sausage maker
Lea Hawkins	42	Georgia	Augusta	3	Seamstress
James Collins	35	Georgia	Augusta	35	Seamstress
Betsy Kelly	27	Georgia	Augusta	22	Washer

Name	Age	Nativity	Residence	How long in Georgia	Occupation
William Hill	45	Virginia	Augusta	37	Barber
Patsy Hill	42	Virginia	Augusta	37	Seamstress
Lewis Brux	11	Georgia	Augusta	11	Apprentice to barber
Jack Carnes	24	South Carolina	Augusta	21	Boatman
Vienna Kelly	27	Augusta	Augusta	27	Seamstress & washer
Jane Scott	23	Georgia	Augusta	23	Seamstress
Patsey Commander	23	South Carolina	Augusta	8	Seamstress
Susan Commander	20	South Carolina	Augusta	8	Seamstress
Matilda Commander	51	South Carolina	Augusta	8	Seamstress
Mary Commander	25	South Carolina	Augusta	8	Seamstress
Eliza Commander	12	South Carolina	Augusta	8	Seamstress
Oliver Antony	33	Lincoln County, Georgia	Augusta	33	Carpenter
Lear Larry	28	Georgia	Augusta	28	Seamstress
Katy Larry	24	Georgia	Augusta	24	Seamstress
York Fleming	25	Georgia	Augusta	25	Cooper
Moses Sparrow	29	Norfolk, Virginia	Augusta	6	House carpenter
Willis Carter	31	North	Augusta	23	House

Name	Age	Nativity	Residence	How long in Georgia	Occupation
		Carolina			carpenter
Jenny Keating	40	Virginia	Augusta	31	Seamstress & washer
Polly Keating	17	Augusta	Augusta	17	Seamstress
Betsy Keating	16	Augusta	Augusta	16	Seamstress
Augustus Keating	5	Augusta	Augusta	5	
Tho Keating	9	Augusta	Augusta	9	
Robert Keating	20	Months	Augusta	20 months	
Adeline Keating	10	months	Augusta	10 months	
Maria Monroe	25	Augusta	Augusta	25	Seamstress & washing
Lewis Monroe	5	Augusta	Augusta		Minor
Mary Monroe	4	Augusta	Augusta		Minor
John Monroe	3	Augusta	Augusta		Minor
Jacob Dent	33	Maryland	Augusta	13	Carpenter
Cloe Dent	27	Maryland	Augusta	13	Seamstress
Laura Dent	19	Maryland	Augusta	2	Seamstress
Roderick Dent	30	Maryland	Augusta	24	Coachman
Milley Sibbles	47	Maryland	Augusta	22	Washer & ironer
Isaac Sibbald	21	Augusta	Augusta	21	laborer
James Triplett	70	Virginia	Augusta	14 years	Wagoner
Richard Triplett	17	Virginia	Augusta	13	Wagoner

51

Name	Age	Nativity	Residence	How long in Georgia	Occupation
Maria Triplett	4	Augusta	Augusta	4	
Alec Pope	42	Pennsylvania	Augusta	20	Drayman
Isabella Lamar	25	Georgia	Augusta	25	Seamstress
Milly Brown	33	Virginia	Augusta	20	Seamstress
Ursla Stith	26	North Carolina	Augusta	19	Washer & seamstress
Shadrack Casey	31	Pennsylvania	Augusta	6	Brick layer
Sarah Johnson	23	Augusta	Augusta	23	Seamstress
William Johnson	6	Augusta	Augusta	6	
James Johnson	5	Augusta	Augusta	5	
John Johnson	1	Augusta	Augusta	1	
George Kelly, dead		Augusta	Augusta		painter
Myra Dent	23	Maryland	Augusta	20	Seamstress, entered the 24th July 1824

Returns for 1825

The original table has no column headings, but appears to contain the same information as in previous years. The table has an extra column that contains no information and is not reproduced in the following transcription.

Name	Age	Nativity	Residence	How long in Georgia	Occupation
Janet Collins	36	Augusta	Augusta	36	Seamstress
Sarah Carnes	41	North Carolina	Augusta	23	Seamstress
Viana Carnes	17	Augusta	Augusta	17	Seamstress
Judi Kelly	40	Augusta	~~South Carolina~~ Augusta	33	Blacksmith
William Kelly	17	South Carolina	Augusta		Blacksmith
Madison Kelly	15	Georgia	Augusta	15	
Augustus Kelly	13	Georgia	Augusta	13	
Ann Kelly	10	Georgia	Augusta	10	
Emily Kelly	8	Georgia	Augusta	8	
John Kelly	13	Georgia	Augusta	13	
Gad Stith	32	Georgia	Augusta	12	Carpenter
Ursile Stith	27	North Carolina	Augusta	19	Seamstress
Thomas Carter	31	Maryland	Augusta	14	Carpenter not paid
Oliver Antony	34	Lincoln County	Augusta	33	Carpenter
Lucy Carnes	25	South Carolina	Augusta	25	Seamstress

Name	Age	Nativity	Residence	How long in Georgia	Occupation
Ja Carnes	5	Augusta	Augusta	5	
Francis Carnes	1	Augusta	Augusta	1	
Jinny Walton	48	Georgia	Augusta	40	Cake baker
Figenia Smith	5	Augusta	Augusta	5	
Turner Smith	25	Wilkes	Augusta	22	Barber & fifer
Matilda Commander	52	South Carolina	Augusta	8	Seamstress
Mary Commander	26	South Carolina	Augusta	8	Seamstress
Patsey Commander	24	South Carolina	Augusta	8	Seamstress
Susan Commander	21	South Carolina	Augusta	8	Seamstress
Eliza Commander	13	South Carolina	Augusta	8	Seamstress
John Commander	11 mos	Augusta	Augusta	11 months	
Mary Ann Johnson	5	Augusta	Augusta	5	
Thomas Parris	55	Augusta	Augusta	55	Boatman
Rachel Chavers	35	South Carolina	Augusta		Washer
Edm^d Chaves	6	Augusta	Augusta	6	
Caty Lary	25	Augusta	Augusta	25	Weaver
Leah Lary	30	Augusta	Augusta	30	Seamstress
Bob Martin	29	Augusta	Augusta	29	Laborer

Name	Age	Nativity	Residence	How long in Georgia	Occupation
H. Williams	32	South Carolina	Augusta	32	Seamstress & weaver
A. Pope	33	Pennsylvania	Augusta	26	Drayman
Amy Ann Daubins	35	South Carolina	Augusta	9	Cook
Syvastin Daubins	9	South Carolina	Augusta	9	Cook
Edinbarrough Daubins	7	South Carolina	Augusta	9	Cook

Returns for 1826

Name	Age	Former Residence	Nativity	Age when Arrived in Georgia	Occupation
Judy Kelly	41	South Carolina		33	
Madison Kelly	16	Georgia			Blacksmith
Augustus Kelly	14	Georgia			
Emily Kelly	9	Georgia			
John Kelly	14	Georgia			
Bob Martin	29	Georgia			Laborer
Milly Brown	32	Virginia		26 years	Seamstress
Tom Parris	56	Georgia		56 years	Boatman
Amy Dobbins	39	South Carolina	Augusta	11 years	Nurse & washer
Laura Dent	22	Georgia	Augusta		Seamstress
Sarah Carnes	42	North Carolina	Augusta	36	Seamstress
V. Carnes	18	Augusta	Augusta	18	Seamstress
L. Carnes	26	South Carolina	Augusta	25	Seamstress
Ja^s Carnes	6	Augusta	Augusta	6	A boy
F. Carnes	2	Augusta	Augusta	2	A girl infant
Milly Sibbald	49	Maryland	Augusta	24	A washer
Isaac Sibbald	23	Augusta	Augusta	23	Boat hand
Patience Todd	56	Virginia	Richmond County	40	Baker

Margaret Todd	5	Georgia	Richmond County	5	

Returns for 1827

The original table has no column headings, but appears to contain the same information as in most previous years.

Name	Age	Nativity	Residence	How long in Georgia	Occupation
Bob Martin	30	Georgia	Georgia		Laborer
Laur Dent	23	Georgia	Georgia		Seamstress
Sarah Carnes	43	North Carolina	Georgia	37	Seamstress
Varna Carnes	19	Augusta	Georgia	19	Seamstress
Milly Sibbald	50	Maryland	Georgia	25	Washer
Isaac Sibbald	24	Augusta	Georgia	24	Boat hand
Lucy Carnes	27	South Carolina	Georgia	25	Seamstress
Ja^s Carnes	7	Augusta	Georgia	7	Boy
F. Carnes	3	Augusta	Georgia	3	A girl infant

Returns for May 1836

Note the different column headings from previous lists. The clerk entered numerous remarks in various columns, all of which are included in the column labeled Remarks.

Name	Age	Former Residence	Nativity	Residence	Remarks
Rachael Chavers	60	South Carolina	South Carolina	Augusta	Washer
Edmund Chavers	18	Augusta	Augusta		An apprentice to bricklayer P. Crump. Registration granted on account of former.
John Wright					Planter. Granted for ditto.
Betsey Kelly	40				Washer. Granted for same.
Sam' Kelly	23	Augusta	Augusta		Idiot
Josiah Kelly	19	Augusta			Blacksmith
Margaret Kelly	16	Augusta			Seamstress. Passed.
Harrington Kelly	14	Augusta			Black. Passed.
Marthena Kelly	11	Augusta			Passed.
John Kelly	6 mos	Augusta			Passed.
Roderick Dent	43	Augusta			Passed.
Cloe Dent	13				Withdrawn
Laura Dent	11				Withdrawn
Sarah Ann Dent	8				Withdrawn

Name	Age	Former Residence	Nativity	Residence	Remarks
Cloe Dent	41				Washer & ironer. Passed on ofc former registry.
Henrietta Dent	15				Passed on affidavit Doc[t] John Dent.
James Dent	13				Passed on affidavit Doc[t] John Dent.
John Dent	11				Passed on affidavit Doc[t] John Dent.
Susan Dent, dead	7				Passed on affidavit Doc[t] John Dent.
Laura Dent	31				Passed, having been registered.
W[m] Dent	7				Passed on oath of Doc[t] Dent.
Mary Mullen	24				Washer & waiter, with a scar over the left eye brow, & left hand little finger much bent. Passed, evidence on file.
Matilda Commander	63	South Carolina			Passed, on former registry.
Mary Commander	38	South Carolina			Seamstress. Passed, on former registry.
Eliza Commander	25	South Carolina			Seamstress. Passed, on former registry.

Name	Age	Former Residence	Nativity	Residence	Remarks
Patsey Commander	36	South Carolina			Seamstress. Passed, on former registry.
Susan Commander	33	South Carolina			Seamstress. Passed, on former registry.
John Commander	12	South Carolina			Child of Martha. Passed on oath of Ge° M. Walker.
George Commander	10 mos				Child of Susan. Passed on oath of Ge° M. Walker.
Matilda Commander, J^r	5½				Child of Susan. Passed on oath of Ge° M. Walker.
Nelly Kelly	44	Augusta			On registry.
Judy Kelly	50	South Carolina	Augusta	Augusta	Washer & ironer. Former registry. These, with the three following, sometimes called Beneful, that being the name of the father.
William Kelly	28	Augusta	Augusta	Augusta	Blacksmith. Passed, former registry. These, with the three following, sometimes called Beneful, that being the name of the father.
Madison Kelly	26	Augusta	Augusta	Augusta	Blacksmith. Passed, former registry. These,

Name	Age	Former Residence	Nativity	Residence	Remarks
					with the three following, sometimes called Beneful, that being the name of the father.
Augustus Kelly	23	Augusta	Augusta	Augusta	Harness maker. Passed, former registry. These, with the three following, sometimes called Beneful, that being the name of the father.
Ann Kelly	21	Augusta	Augusta	Augusta	Washer. Passed, former registry. These, with the three following, sometimes called Beneful, that being the name of the father.
Emily Kelly	19	Augusta	Augusta	Augusta	Seamstress. Passed, former registry. These, with the three following, sometimes called Beneful, that being the name of the father.
John Kelly	24	Augusta	Augusta	Augusta	Washer. Passed, former registry. These, with the three following, sometimes called Beneful, that

Name	Age	Former Residence	Nativity	Residence	Remarks
					being the name of the father.
Laura L. Kelly	11	Augusta	Augusta	Augusta	Washer & Seamstress. Passed, former registry. These, with the three following, sometimes called Beneful, that being the name of the father.
Eliza Kelly	11 mos				Passed on oath of D. Morrison. Passed on evidence on file.
Henry Kelly	3				Passed on oath of D. Morrison. Passed on evidence on file.
James Kelly	8				Passed on oath of D. Morrison. Passed on evidence on file.
Matilda Bowers	25				Seamstress. Passed on evidence of U. B. Clark.
John M. Bowers	5				Passed on evidence of U. B. Clark & H. Aldrich.
Mary Ann Johnson	16				Passed on evidence of M. R. Martin.

Name	Age	Former Residence	Nativity	Residence	Remarks
Jacob Dent	45				Passed, former registry.
Myra Dent	32				Passed, former registry.
Thomas Dent	13				Passed, on affidavit of Doc^t Jno Dent.
Henry Dent	11				Passed, on affidavit of Doc^t Jno Dent.
Elizabeth Dent	6				Passed, on affidavit of Doc^t Jno Dent.
Sandy Dent	18 mos				Passed, on affidavit of Doc^t Jno Dent.
Juno Kelly	37	Augusta	Augusta	37 years	Black complexion. Washer woman. Passed, on former registry.
Ned Kelly, son of above	11	Augusta	Augusta	11	Black complexion. Washer. Passed, on former registry.
Martha Kelly	13	Augusta	Augusta		Black complexion. Passed, on former registry.
Alfred Kelly	18	Augusta	Augusta	18	Yellow complexion. Drayman. Passed, on former

Name	Age	Former Residence	Nativity	Residence	Remarks
					registry.
Rebecca Kelly	32	Augusta	Augusta	32	Yellow complexion. Washer. Passed, on former registry.
Eliza Kelly	29	Augusta	Augusta	29	Yellow complexion. Washer. Passed, on former registry.
Martha Kelly	26	Augusta	Augusta	26	Yellow complexion. Washer. Passed, on former registry.
Barbary Kelly	40	Augusta	Augusta	40	Black complexion. Washer. Passed, on former registry.
Isaac Kelly	18	Augusta	Augusta	18	Black complexion. Washer. Passed, on former registry.
John A. Kelly	16	Augusta	Augusta	16	Children of above. Passed, on former registry.
Nancy Kelly	10	Augusta	Augusta	10	Children of above. Passed, on former registry.
Elizabeth Kelly	8	Augusta	Augusta	8	Children of above. Passed, on former registry.

Name	Age	Former Residence	Nativity	Residence	Remarks
Maria Bush	25				Passed, having shown evidence of registry in Burke County.
Isaiah Bush	6				Child of above. Passed, having shown evidence of registry in Burke County.
Mary Ann Jones Moore	23				Children of Ellen Jones. Passed on oath of Tarpin, on file.
Hannah Jones Moore	1				Mary A. Jones or Moore child.
Harriet Lloyd	31				A washer & seamstress. Wife to Wm Kelly. Passed on evidence on file.
Jane A. Lloyd	12				Now in Sav^h.
Wm A. Lloyd	4 mos				Passed on evidence on file.
Peter Johnson	32				Passed, on former registry.
Jane Johnson	16				Passed, on former registry.
Ann Johnson	14				Passed, on former registry.
Malinda Johnson	12				Passed, on former registry.
Nancy Johnson	55				Passed, on former registry.

Name	Age	Former Residence	Nativity	Residence	Remarks
Josiah Brown	39				Passed, on evidence on file in Clerk's office.
Sally Johnson	42				Passed.
Henry Kelly	20				Passed, on proof of former registry.
~~Sarah Todd~~	27				Withdrawn. Wife and children of Peter Johnson.
~~Margaret Todd~~	5				Withdrawn
~~Peter Todd~~	3				Withdrawn
~~Maria Todd~~	1				Withdrawn
Polly Gantt	40				Washer. Passed, on proof former registry in Lincoln County.
Jordan Gantt	23				Waiter. Children of above, as p[r] evidence on file & passed by the Court.
Mary Gantt	10				Children of above, as p[r] evidence on file & passed by the Court.
Amanda Gantt	9				Children of above, as p[r] evidence on file & passed by the Court.
William Gantt	2				Children of above, as p[r] evidence on file & passed by the Court.

67

Name	Age	Former Residence	Nativity	Residence	Remarks
Lucy Carnes	40	South Carolina	Augusta	Augusta	Washer & iron. Passed, on former registry.
Sarah Carnes	12				Passed, as children of above.
Francis Carnes	13				Passed, as children of above.
Elizabeth Carnes	10				Passed, as children of above.
James Carnes	15				Passed, as children of above.
Lucy Carnes	5				Passed, as children of above.
Vienna Carnes	30				Passed, on proof of former registry.
Sarah Carnes	8				Passed, as children of above.
Simeon Carnes	17 mos				Passed, as children of above.
Milley Sibbald	59				Passed, on proof of former registry.
Jane Sibbald	32				Passed, on proof of former registry.
Mansa Sibbald	29				Passed, on proof of former registry.
Wm Sibbald	22				Passed, on proof of former registry.
Edmund Sibbald	4				
Charles Sibbald	23				Passed, on proof of former registry.

Name	Age	Former Residence	Nativity	Residence	Remarks
Virginia Sibbald	8 wks				Child of Jane Sibbald, passed.
Elizabeth Lee	25				Seamstress, washer, & ironer. Passed, on testimony of Ge° M. Walker.
Adaline Lett	25	Hancock County	Augusta	Augusta	Washer & ironer. Passed, on proof of registry in Hancock County.
Willis Lett	22	Hancock County	Augusta	Augusta	Blacksmith. Passed, on proof of registry in Hancock County.
Martha Lett	20	Hancock County	Augusta	Augusta	Washer. Passed, on proof of registry in Hancock County.
Richmond Lett	16	Hancock County	Augusta	Augusta	Blacksmith, trade apprentice. Passed, on proof of registry in Hancock County.
William Lett	13			Augusta	Blacksmith, trade apprentice. Children & born since the above registry.
Royell Lett	12			Augusta	Children & born since the above registry.
Georgeann Lett	8			Augusta	Child of Adeline. Children & born since the above

Name	Age	Former Residence	Nativity	Residence	Remarks
					registry.
Tho[s] C. Bonneau	22				Passed, on evidence on file with the Clerk.
John Scott	22				The Court, in these three cases, issues their opinion giving the parties time to procure further testimony.
Harrison Scott	20				The Court, in these three cases, issues their opinion giving the parties time to procure further testimony.
Nancy Scott	17				The Court, in these three cases, issues their opinion giving the parties time to procure further testimony.
Martisia Caroline, or Fitz	23				
Jeremiah Caroline, or Fitz	5				
Amy Dobbins	50				Washer & ironer. Passed, on proof of former registry.
Sylvester Dobbins	22				Cabinet maker. Passed, on proof of former registry.

Name	Age	Former Residence	Nativity	Residence	Remarks
Edinborough Dobbins	17				Waiter. Passed, on proof of former registry.
Gad Stith	43				Carpenter. passed, on proof of registry formerly.
Ursula Stith	39				Passed, on proof of former registry.
William Sibbald	22				Passed, on proof of former registry.
~~Charles Sibbald~~	~~23~~				
Isaac Sibbald	30				Passed, on proof of former registry.
Louisa Sibbald	19				Passed, on proof of former registry.
Jane Sibbald	32				Passed, on proof of former registry.
Milley Sibbald	11				Child of Jane, passed.
William Sibbald	8				Child of Jane, passed.
Edmund Sibbald	4				Child of Jane, passed.
Charles Sibbald	2				Child of Jane, passed.
Virginia Sibbald	8 mos				Child of Jane, passed.
George Grant	46				Continued by the Court to allow the applicant to procure proof.

71

Name	Age	Former Residence	Nativity	Residence	Remarks
					Passed. on proof of former registry.
Jack Carnes	31				Passed, on proof of former registry.
Joe Carnes	40				Passed, on proof of former registry.
Jeffrey Moore	45				Passed, on proof on file.
Diana Kelly	7				Passed, as the child of Betsey Kelly.
~~Samuel Kelly~~	~~22~~				
Nancy Martin	26				Their cases are reserved by the Court for further proof of freedom.
James Martin	25				Their cases are reserved by the Court for further proof of freedom.
Bob Martin	40				Passed, on proof of former registry.
John Clesby	27				Passed, on proof of former registry.
Caroline Clesby	10				Child of above.
Isabella Woodson, or Moon	45				Passed, on proof of former registry.
Polly Bush, alias Millen	45	South Carolina	Augusta	Augusta	Seamstress & washer. Passed before.

Name	Age	Former Residence	Nativity	Residence	Remarks
James Bush, alias Millen	14	Burke County	Augusta	Augusta	Barber. Passed before.
Mary Ann Millen	16	Burke County	Augusta	Augusta	Seamstress. Passed before.
David Bush, alias Millen	12	Burke County	Augusta	Augusta	Waiter. Passed before.
Richard Bush, alias Millen	8	Burke County	Augusta	Augusta	Passed before.
Jane Bush, alias Millen	7	Burke County	Augusta	Augusta	Passed before.
Virginia Bush, alias Millen	5	Burke County	Augusta	Augusta	Passed before.
Milly Brown					Passed, as formerly registered.
Elizabeth Martin	14	Augusta			Reserved by the Court for further proof of freedom.
Jane Scott, or Kelly	35	Augusta			Passed, on proof of former registry.
Alex^r Scott	3	Augusta			Passed, as children of Jane.
Wm H. Scott	5 mos	Augusta			Passed, as children of Jane.
Betsy McFarlane	50	Augusta			Washer & ironer. Passed, on proof of former registry.
Eliza Keating	28	Augusta			Passed, on proof of former registry.
Polly Keating	29	Augusta			Passed, on proof of former registry.

Name	Age	Former Residence	Nativity	Residence	Remarks
Martha Keating	21	Augusta			Passed, on proof of former registry.
Thomas Keating	18	Augusta			Brother of above girls
Robert Keating	12	Augusta			Son of Polly.
Adeline Keating	11	Augusta			Child of Eliza.
Elizabeth Keating	10	Augusta			Child of Eliza.
Patsey Keating	76	Augusta			Passed, on proof of former registry.
~~Betsey McFarland~~	~~55~~	Augusta			
Viney Hawkins	42	Augusta			Passed, on proof of former registry in Chatham County.
Betsy Coleman	40	Augusta			Wife & daughter of John Coleman. Passed on filing with the Clerk the necessary proof.
Susan Coleman	18	Augusta			Wife & daughter of John Coleman. Passed on filing with the Clerk the necessary proof.
James Evans	25	Augusta			Passed, on proof of former registry.
John Haynes	41	Augusta			Free act of Legislature.
Francis Haynes	49	Augusta			Free by act of Legislature.

Name	Age	Former Residence	Nativity	Residence	Remarks
Alex Pope	65				Passed, on proof of former registry.
Polly Wright					Passed, on proof of former registry.
James Triplett					Passed, on proof of former registry.
Aaron Keating					Passed, on proof of former registry.
Ellen Rouse, or Knight	52				Passed, on proof of former registry.
Priscilla Evans, or Bing	56				Washer & C. Passed, on proof of former registry.
Anthony Haynes	44				Free by act of the Legislature.
Ann Scott, or Rouse	20				Seamstress. Child of Vicey Rouse. Passed
Vicey Rouse	54				Passed, on proof of former registry.
John Rouse	24				Passed. Child of Vicey.
William Hill	57	Virginia			Barber
Catherine Simons	24				Suspended until the opinion of Judge Holt is obtained on the obedience.
Sarah Thomas, alias Fitch	51				
Andrew Thomas, alias					

Name	Age	Former Residence	Nativity	Residence	Remarks
Fitch					
Billy Hoxey	55	Georgia			Carpenter. Passed on proof on file.
Lufaney Hoxey	34	Georgia			Seamstress. Passed on proof on file.
Mary Hoxey	14	Georgia			Seamstress. Passed on proof on file.
Sarah Hoxey	12	Georgia			Passed on proof on file.
Betsy A. Hoxey	10	Georgia	Wilkes County	Augusta	Passed on proof on file.
Caroline Hoxey	8	Georgia			An idiot. Passed on proof on file.
Wm H. Haey	4				Passed on proof on file.
Josephine Hoxey	4 mos				Passed on proof on file.
Edmund Hall	20		Jefferson County	Richmond County	Upon the oath of Judge J. Shly.
Jim Kelly	48		Augusta		Blacksmith. Former registry.
Nelly Jones	47		Virginia	Augusta	Washer. Former registry.
Mary Monroe, or Page	16		Augusta	Augusta	Upon affidavit of their being the children of Maria Monroe, who was formerly registered.

Name	Age	Former Residence	Nativity	Residence	Remarks
John Monroe, or Page	15				Upon affidavit of their being the children of Maria Monroe, who was formerly registered.
William Henry, or Page	13				Upon affidavit of their being the children of Maria Monroe, who was formerly registered.
David Scott	20		Richmond County		Passed, on oath of John Chavers
John Cosins	71		Virginia		Passed, on former registry.
Sarah Fitz	47		South Carolina	-	Washer. Passed, on former registry.
Andrew Fitz	17		Augusta		Field hand. Passed, on former registry.
Martha Collins	29		Burke County		Seamstress
John Collins	16		Burke County		Hostler
Jane Collins	8		Burke County		
Jesse Collins	6		Burke County		

Returns for 1843

The original table has no column headings and contains much less information that previous lists.

Name	Age	Remarks	Occupation
Polly Gantt	48	Passed on proof before the Court, see 1836.	Washer
Jordan Gantt	30	Children in proof, as per evidence passed by Court.	Carpenter
Mary Gantt	17		
Amanda Gantt	15		
William Gant	9		
Thomas Gant	5		

Returns for July 1844

Name	Age	Former Residence	Nativity	Present Residence	Remarks
Polly Gantt	49	Lincoln County	Maryland	Augusta	On former evidence.
Jordan Gantt	31	Lincoln County	Lincoln County	Augusta	Children of Polly Gantt and passed on former registry.
Mary Gantt	18	Augusta	Augusta	Augusta	Children of Polly Gantt and passed on former registry.
Amanda Gantt	16	Augusta	Augusta	Augusta	Children of Polly Gantt and passed on former registry.
William Gantt	10	Augusta	Augusta	Augusta	Children of Polly Gantt and passed on former registry.
Thomas Gantt	6	Augusta	Augusta	Augusta	Children of Polly Gantt and passed on former registry.
Laura Kelly	29	Augusta	Augusta	Augusta	Passed on former registry.
Henry Kelly	11	Augusta	Augusta	Augusta	Passed on former registry.
[blank] Kelly	9	Augusta	Augusta	Augusta	Passed on former registry.
Gad Stith	54	Augusta	Augusta	Augusta	Passed on former registry.
Ursule Stith	46	Augusta	Augusta	Augusta	Passed on former registry.

Name	Age	Former Residence	Nativity	Present Residence	Remarks
Josephine Stith	14	Augusta	Augusta	Augusta	Passed on former registry.
Martha Collins	37	Burke County	Burke County	Burke County	Passed on former registry.
John Collins	20	Burke County	Burke County	Burke County	Passed on former registry.
Jane Collins	14	Burke County	Burke County	Burke County	Passed on former registry.
Jesse Collins	12	Burke County	Burke County	Burke County	Passed on former registry.
Sarah Carnes	42	Richmond County	Richmond County	Burke County	
Vienna Carnes	40	Augusta	Augusta	Augusta	Seamstress. Appeared on former registry.
Sarah Carnes	16	Augusta	Augusta	Augusta	Appeared on former registry.
Simeon Carnes	9½	Augusta	Augusta	Augusta	Appeared on former registry.
Peter Johnson	40	Augusta	Augusta	Augusta	Blacksmith. Passed, on former registry.
Josiah Kelly	27	Augusta	Augusta	Augusta	Passed, on former registry.
Harrington Kelly	22	Augusta	Augusta	Augusta	Passed, on former registry.
Betsy Kelly	48	Augusta	Augusta	Augusta	Washer & ironer. Passed, on former registry.
Martha Keating	29	Augusta	Augusta	Augusta	Passed, on

Name	Age	Former Residence	Nativity	Present Residence	Remarks
					former registry.
Diannah Kelly	29	Augusta	Augusta	Augusta	Passed, on former registry.
Martha Kelly	21	Augusta	Augusta	Augusta	Passed, on former registry.
Margaretta Kelly	24	Augusta	Augusta	Augusta	Passed, on former registry.
Marthena Kelly	19	Augusta	Augusta	Augusta	Passed, on former registry.
Juno Kelly	45	Augusta	Augusta	Augusta	Passed, on former registry.
Sarah Kelly	7	Augusta	Augusta	Augusta	The daughter of Margarett Kelly.
Thomas Kelly	5	Augusta	Augusta	Augusta	The son of Margarett Kelly.
Eliza Kelly	3	Augusta	Augusta	Augusta	The daughter of Margarett Kelly.
Lavinia Kelly	4 mos	Augusta	Augusta	Augusta	The daughter of Margarett Kelly.
John Clesby	~~23~~ 47	New York	34 years of age		Passed, on former registry.
Caroline Clesby	18		18 years of age		Passed, on former registry.
Malinda Johnson	20	Augusta			Passed, on former registry.
Jane Johnson	24				

Name	Age	Former Residence	Nativity	Present Residence	Remarks
Ann Johnson	22				
Nancy Johnson	13				
Lucy Carnes	48	South Carolina			Passed, on former registry.
Matilda Bowers	33	Augusta			Of light complexion. Passed, on former registry.
James M. Bowers	13				Of light complexion. Passed, on former registry.
Sarah Carnes	20				
Francis Carnes	21				A free boy.
Elizabeth Carnes	18				
James Carnes	23				
Lucy Carnes	13				
Jeffrey Moore	53				Passed, on former registry.
Isabella Woodson, or Moore	49 53				Passed, on former registry.
Jane Sibbald	40				Black complexion.
Milly Sibbald	19				Yellowish complexion. Children of Jane. Apprentices to tradesmen & traders.

Name	Age	Former Residence	Nativity	Present Residence	Remarks
William Sibbald	16				Yellowish complexion. Children of Jane. Apprentices to tradesmen & traders.
Edmund Sibbald	12				Yellowish complexion. Children of Jane. Apprentices to tradesmen & traders.
Charles Sibbald	10				Yellowish complexion. Children of Jane. Apprentices to tradesmen & traders.
Virginia Sibbald	9				Yellowish complexion. Children of Jane. Apprentices to tradesmen & traders.
Louisa Sibbald	27				Black
James Sibbald	4				Black
Edward Sibbald	2				Black
Darias Armond	31		South Carolina		Yellowish complexion. On evidence of record in Book T, folio 236, & on oath John

Name	Age	Former Residence	Nativity	Present Residence	Remarks
					Guemarin.
Qu[blot] Armond	29				Yellowish complexion.
William Armond	9				Yellowish complexion. Waiter. Son of Darias. Children of Quilly.
Augustus Armond	10				Yellowish complexion. Children of Quilly.
Sarah Jane Armond	6				Yellowish complexion. Children of Quilly.
Elizabeth Posa	2				Yellowish complexion. On evidence.
Cecile Charles, the daughter of Charlotte Corregoles	26				Of Indian complexion. A native of Savannah. Seamstress. On evidence.
Martha Lett	28				Washer & ironer. Passed on proof.
Henry Lett	6				Children of Martha Lett.
Betsy Lett	4				Children of Martha Lett.

Name	Age	Former Residence	Nativity	Present Residence	Remarks
Laura Lett	6 mos				Children of Martha Lett.
Royall Lett	20				Blacksmith
Rachael Chavers	68				
Edmund Chavers	26				
Laura Chavers, formerly Laura Dent					
Cloe Dent					
Edmund Chavers					
Mathew Harman	50				
Phillis Russell	70				Laborer. Passed, on evidence of Mr Green, the guardian, Richmond County.
Palmon Russell	35				Drayman Children of Phillis.
Abiah Russell	20				Drayman. Children of Phillis.
Morris Russell	18				Laborer. Children of Phillis.
David Russell	16				Laborer. Children of Phillis.

Name	Age	Former Residence	Nativity	Present Residence	Remarks
Adolphus Russell	7				Betsy Russell
Henry Kelly	28				Drayman. Passed, on evidence of former registry.
Eliza Kelly	37				Yellowish complexion. On former registry.
William Kelly	36				On former registry.
Harriet Lloyd	39				The wife & children of William Kelly & entered on former registry.
Jane A. Lloyd	20				
Wm A. Lloyd	8½				
Willis Lett	30				
Georgeanna	16				
William Lett	21				
Richmond Lett	24				
~~Billy Hoxey~~	~~63~~				
Lufany Hoxey	42				
Mary Hoxey	22				
Julia Hoxey	2				
Wm H. Hoxey	12½				

Name	Age	Former Residence	Nativity	Present Residence	Remarks
Josephine Hoxey	9				
Lloyd Hoxey	5				
Corenthia Hoxey	2				
Miflin Hoxey	1				
Sarah Hoxey	20				
Robert Keating	21				Passed, on former registry.
~~William Henry~~	~~63~~				
Charles Sabald	40				Passed, on former registry.

Passed in Inferior Court Sep Term 1847

At Sup Court June Term, see minutes.

Ester Sills

John Scott & wife

Emily Kelly

Third Register, 1848-1863

The following transcriptions consist of a series of tables with six columns, usually including the name of the registrant, their age, occupation, residence, name of their guardian, and year of registration.

Returns for 1848

The remarks column combines two columns in the original, one titled how passed and the other occupation or pursuit. That table has two pages. On the third page, the how passed column is changed to names of guardians.

A List of Free Persons of Color Registered for the Year 1848

Name	Age	Nativity	Residence	Time of Coming into State	Remarks
Richmond Lett	26	Hancock County	Augusta		
Royell Lett	23	Augusta	Augusta	At birth, but registry of mother in Hancock County.	Blacksmith. Passed on Proof.
Georgeanna	19	Augusta	Augusta	At birth.	Washer. Passed on proof.
Martha Lett	30	Hancock County	Augusta	At birth.	Washer & ironer. Passed on proof.
Henry Lett	9	Augusta	Augusta	At birth.	Son of Martha Lett. Passed on Proof.
Patsey Lett	7	Augusta	Augusta	At birth.	Daughter of Martha Lett. Passed on proof.
Laura Lett	4	Augusta	Augusta	At birth.	Daughter of Martha Lett. Passed on proof.
Royell Lett	2	Augusta	Augusta	At birth.	Son of Martha Lett. Passed on Proof.
Anna Kelly	32	Augusta	Augusta	At Augusta, mother free.	Washer & ironer.

Name	Age	Nativity	Residence	Time of Coming into State	Remarks
					Passed on proof.
Henry Raymond Kelly	15	Augusta	Augusta	At Augusta, mother free.	Son of Anna Kelly. Barber, by trade. Passed on proof.
Eliza Ann Kelly	13	Augusta	Augusta	At Augusta, mother free.	Daughter of Anna Kelly. Seamstress. Passed on proof.
Lufeny Hoxey	47	~~Washington,~~ Wilkes Columbia County	Augusta	Washington	Daughter of Lufeney Hoxey. Seamstress. Passed on proof.
Mary Hoxey	25	~~Washington,~~ Wilkes Columbia County	Augusta	Washington	
Julia Hoxey	6	Augusta	Augusta	Augusta	Daughter of Mary Hoxey. Passed on proof.
Augustus Hoxey	3	Augusta	Augusta	Augusta	Son of Mary Hoxey. Passed on proof.
Louisa Hoxey	13 mos	Augusta	Augusta	Augusta	Daughter of Mary Hoxey. Passed on proof.
Margaretta Kelly	27	Augusta	Augusta	Augusta	Daughter of Betsy Kelly. Washer & ironer. Passed on proof.
Sarah Kelly	10	Augusta	Augusta	Augusta	Passed on proof.
Thomas Kelly	8	Augusta	Augusta	Augusta	Passed on proof.

Name	Age	Nativity	Residence	Time of Coming into State	Remarks
Mary Eliza Kelly	6	Augusta	Augusta	Augusta	Passed on proof.
Harrison Kelly, dead	4	Augusta	Augusta	Augusta	Passed on proof.
Anna Margarett Kelly, dead	2 mos	Augusta	Augusta	~~Augusta~~ Washington	Passed on proof.
Sarah Hoxey	23	Augusta	Augusta	Augusta	Nurse. Passed on proof.
William Hoxey	16	Augusta	Augusta	Augusta	Carpenter. Passed on proof.
Josephine Hoxey	12	Augusta	Augusta	Augusta	Nurse. Passed on proof.
Lloyd Hoxey	7	Augusta	Augusta	Augusta	Passed on proof.
Corenthia Hoxey	5	Augusta	Augusta	Augusta	Passed on proof.
Mifflin Hoxey	3½	Augusta	Augusta	Augusta	Passed on proof.
Willis Lett	34	Hancock County	Augusta	Augusta	Blacksmith. Passed on proof
Harrington Kelly	26	Augusta	Augusta	Augusta	Blacksmith. Passed on proof
Romulus Corvin	25	Columbia County	Augusta	Augusta	Blacksmith. Light complected. Passed on proof
Elizabeth Corvin	24	Columbia County	Augusta	Augusta	Seamstress. Light complected. Passed on proof.
Laura Corvin	23	Columbia County	Augusta	Augusta	Seamstress. Light complected.

Name	Age	Nativity	Residence	Time of Coming into State	Remarks
					Passed on proof.
William Henry Corvin	2	Richmond County	Augusta	Augusta	Child of Elizabeth Corvin, aged 2½. Passed on proof.
Allen Corvin	3				Child of Elizabeth Corvin, 2 years 29 August last. Passed on proof.
Roderick Dent	55	Maryland	Augusta	Bright mulatto.	Blacksmith. Passed on evidence.
Susan Commander	44	South Carolina	Augusta	Bright mulatto.	Seamstress. Wife of R. Dent. Passed on proof.
George Samuel Commander	13	Augusta	Augusta	Bright mulatto.	Apprentice. Son of R. Dent & Susan Commander.
Mary Jane Commander	7	Augusta	Augusta	Bright mulatto.	Daughter of R. Dent & Susan Commander.
Savannah Matilda Commander	5	Augusta	Augusta	Bright mulatto.	Daughter of R. Dent & Susan Commander.
Martha Ann Commander	2	Augusta	Augusta	Bright mulatto.	Daughter of R. Dent & Susan Commander.
William Henry Dent	8 mos	Augusta	Augusta	Bright mulatto.	The son of Susan Dent, dec[d] & Jordon Jones, in charge of R.

Name	Age	Nativity	Residence	Time of Coming into State	Remarks
					Dent.
John Dent	22	Augusta	Augusta	Bright mulatto.	Blacksmith. The son of Cloe Dent, dec.
Henrietta Dent	26	Augusta	Augusta	Bright mulatto.	Seamstress & general servant. Passed on evidence & daughter of Cloe.
Sarah Harris Dent	4			Dark	The child of Henrietta Dent.
Chloe Ann Dent	1			Darkish color.	The child of Henrietta Dent.
Jordon Gantt	34	Petersburgh, Georgia	Augusta	Mulatto	Carpenter & laborer.
William Henry Gantt	8 mos	Augusta	Augusta	Mulatto	The son of Susan Dent, dec[d] & his father Jordan Gantt
Myra Dent	48	Maryland	Augusta	Mulatto	Seamstress
Thomas Dent	24	Augusta	Augusta	Mulatto	Carpenter. The children of Myra Dent, registered above their names on proof of registry.
Elizabeth Dent	17	Augusta	Augusta	Mulatto	The children of Myra Dent, registered above their names on proof of registry.
Sandy Dent	12	Augusta	Augusta	Mulatto	The children of

Name	Age	Nativity	Residence	Time of Coming into State	Remarks
					Myra Dent, registered above their names on proof of registry.
Sarah Dent	9	Augusta	Augusta	Mulatto	The children of Myra Dent, registered above their names on proof of registry.
John Dent	3	Augusta	Augusta	Mulatto	The children of Myra Dent, registered above their names on proof of registry.

A List of Free Negroes Registered for the Year 1848

Name	Age	Nativity	Time of Coming to Georgia	Guardian	Occupation and Residence
Lucy Carnes	49	South Carolina	15 years of age	Augustus B. Longstreet	Seamstress Augusta
Sarah Carnes	24	Augusta		Augustus B. Longstreet	Seamstress Augusta
Elizabeth Carnes	22	Augusta		Augustus B. Longstreet	Seamstress Augusta
Francis Carnes	23	Augusta		Augustus B. Longstreet	Drayman Augusta
James Carnes	23	Augusta		Augustus B. Longstreet	Drayman Augusta
Lucy Carnes	17	Augusta		Augustus B. Longstreet	Seamstress Augusta
Matilda Bowers	38	Augusta	From birth	John Phinizy	Seamstress Color mulatto Augusta
James M. Bowers	17	Augusta	From birth		Turner Bright mulatto Augusta
Cecile Charles, daughter of Charlotte Corrigoles	30	Savannah	12 years	G. F. Parish	Of bright Indian complexion Augusta
William Cecile	7	Augusta	From birth	G. F. Parish	The children of Cecile Charles
Mary Ann Cecile	3	Augusta	From birth	G. F. Parish	The children of Cecile Charles
Gad Stith, dead	48 55	Georgia	From birth		Carpenter Yellow complexion Augusta

Name	Age	Nativity	Time of Coming to Georgia	Guardian	Occupation and Residence
Ursele Stith	50	North Carolina	From birth		Seamstress Very light complexion Augusta
Diana Kelly	19	Augusta	From birth	Wm R. McLaws	Washer & ironer Augusta
Josephine Stith	18	Augusta	From birth	H. H.	Seamstress Augusta
Fanny Dolly	38	Savannah	3 years in Augusta	Philip McGan	Seamstress Augusta
Ann Scott	28	Richmond County		Jesse Johnson	Washer & seamstress Richmond County
Martha Collins & her	41	Burke County	16 years in Augusta		Seamstress & baker Richmond County
Jesse Collins	16	Burke County			Butcher Richmond County
Jane Collins & her son	18	Burke County	16 years in Augusta		Seamstress, washer, & ironer Richmond County
John	2	Burke County	Richmond		
Laney Young	23	Burke County		Jesse Johnson 25 Feby 1847	Washer & ironer Richmond County

Returns for 1849 & 1850

A List of Free Persons of Color Registered for the Year 1849 & 1850

Name	Age	Nativity	Time of Coming to Georgia	Guardian	Occupation and Residence
James Kelly, alias Benefold	19	Augusta	From birth	Gary F. Parish	The son of Judy Kelly, a free woman of color & duly entered Madison, Morgan County
Laura Corven	25	Born in Columbia County	From birth	J. Thomas Robt Schly	The daughter of Critty Corven Richmond County
William Corvin	29	Born in Columbia County	From birth	J. Muskey	Millwright & farms, 5 ^{12}/inches Richmond County

Returns for 1851

Unless otherwise noted, the clerk entered all the residences as Georgia in the original volume, those entries not repeated here.

Names Registered 1851

Name	Age	Nativity	Time of Coming to Georgia	Guardian	Occupation
William Sibbald	22 16th Jun 1851	Augusta	Certificate granted March	George M. Walker	Car builder & carpenter
Edmund Sibbald	20	Augusta	Certificate granted March	George M. Walker	Wheelwright
John Collins	24	Augusta	Certificate granted March		Blacksmith
Patsey Russell			By order of Court, see minutes.	A. W. Rhodes	
Jane Collins	22	Burke County	Passed on former registry		Seamstress, washer, & ironer & one baby named William, aged 3 months, born 14th Jany 1851
& her sons, John & William	5	Richmond County	Passed on former registry		
Elizabeth Hughes	21	Richmond County	Passed by order of Court		Washer & ironer
Martha Lett	33	Hancock County	Passed on former		Washer & ironer

99

Name	Age	Nativity	Time of Coming to Georgia	Guardian	Occupation
			registry		
Patsey Lett	12	Augusta	Passed on former registry		Children of Martha Lett & her husband George Dill, a blacksmith
Henry Lett	10	Augusta	Passed on former registry		Children of Martha Lett & her husband George Dill, a blacksmith
Laura or Laurey Lett	7	Augusta	Passed on former registry		Children of Martha Lett & her husband George Dill, a blacksmith
Royall Lett	26	Augusta	Passed on former registry		
Peter Johnson	49	Augusta	Passed on former registry		Blacksmith
And his wife Sarah Johnson, formerly Todd & their children	49	Augusta	Passed on former registry		Washer & ironer
Margaret	16	Augusta	Passed on former registry		Seamstress
Peter	15	Augusta	Passed on former registry		Blacksmith
Mariah	14	Augusta	Passed on former		seamstress

Name	Age	Nativity	Time of Coming to Georgia	Guardian	Occupation
			registry		
Henry	12	Augusta	Passed on former registry		
John Johnson	11	Augusta			
David Johnson	10	Augusta			
Billy Johnson	7	Augusta			
Susannah Johnson	4	Augusta			
Nancy Ann Johnson	1	Augusta			
Ann Johnson	35	Augusta			Not of good sense
Emily Kelly	35	Augusta		A. J. Miller	Washer & ironer
Julia Kelly	12	Augusta		A. J. Miller	Child of Emily
Anna Kelly (W^m McCormick)	37	Augusta		Ja^s Gardner, J^r	Washer & ironer
Henry Raymond Kelly	17	Augusta		Ja^s Gardner, J^r	Barber Children of Anna
Eliza Anna Kelly	15	Augusta		Ja^s Gardner, J^r	Children of Anna
Becca Youngblood		Augusta		G.	By order of Court
Augustus Kelly	36	Augusta			Harness maker
Mary Gantt	25	Augusta			Seamstress

Name	Age	Nativity	Time of Coming to Georgia	Guardian	Occupation
Adolphus	4	Augusta			Children of Mary Gantt
Henry	9 mos	Charleston			Children of Mary Gantt
Martha, Charlotte Harris' daughter	30	Savannah			Washer & ironer
Jane Moore	28	Columbia, South Carolina	1846	Gerry F. Parish	Seamstress
Mary Elizabeth Moore	5	Augusta		Gerry F. Parish	
Robert Harper, formerly Robt Keating	28	Augusta		Andrew J. Miller	Piano tuner
Malinda Johnson	26	Augusta		Gerry F. Parish	Seamstress
Jane Sibbald	46	Augusta		Gerry F. Parish	Washer & ironer
Milly Sibbald	24				Children of Jane Sibbald
Charles Sibbald	14				Children of Jane Sibbald
Virginia Sibbald	12				Children of Jane Sibbald
David Sibbald	9				Children of Jane Sibbald
Mary Jane Sibbald	7				Children of Jane Sibbald
Joseph Sibbald	5				Children of Jane

Name	Age	Nativity	Time of Coming to Georgia	Guardian	Occupation
					Sibbald
Emma Louisa Sibbald	3				Children of Jane Sibbald
Lucy Carnes	52	South Carolina			Seamstress
Sarah Carnes	23				
Elizabeth Carnes	25				
Francis Carnes	28				Drayman
James Carnes	30				Drayman
Matilda Bowers	42	South Carolina		Jn° Phinizy	Seamstress
James M. Bowers	17	Augusta		Jn° Hill	Tinner
Catherine Simmons	40	South Carolina		A. J. Miller	Mantua maker
Joseph Kelly	31	South Carolina		Garey F. Parish	Blacksmith
Catherine Simons, child	10	Augusta			Child of Catherine Simons
Mary Hoxie	30	Washington, Wilkes			
Mary Jane Hoxie	3				Children of Mary Hoxie & Rich[d] Williams
Emma Louisa Hoxie	4				Children of Mary Hoxie & Rich[d] Williams

Returns for 1852

The clerk entered Augusta as the residence for all of the registrants.

A List of Free Persons of Color Registered of Year 1852

Name	Age	Nativity	Time of Coming to Georgia	Guardian	Occupation
Ann Kelly, wife of W^m McC.	38			James Gardner, J^r	Washer & ironer
Ann Eliza Kelly	16	Augusta		James Gardner, J^r	Washer & ironer Children of Ann K.
Henry Raymond Kelly	18	Augusta		James Gardner, J^r	Barber Children of Ann K.
Clement Sabatti	23	Chatham County	1851	Samuel H. Crump	Barber
Romulus Corvin	30	Columbia County		No guardian	Blacksmith
Elizabeth Hughes	22	Augusta		Jesse Osmond	Washer & ironer
Josiah Brown	30	Augusta		James Harper	Bricklayer
Susan Todd	35	Augusta		Jonathan Miller	

Returns for 1854

A List of Free persons of Color Registered of Year 1854

Name	Age	Nativity	Time of Coming to Georgia	Guardian	Occupation, Residence, and Date of Registration
Samuel Burnett	49	Warren County	Born in Georgia	T. F. Persons	Laborer Richmond County 28 Jan 1854
Rebecca Jane Burnett	44	Warren County	Born in Georgia	T. F. Persons	Richmond County 28 Jan 1854
Elixena Burnett	12	Warren County	Born in Georgia	T. F. Persons	Richmond County 28 Jan 1854
Loidane Burnett	8	Warren County	Born in Georgia	T. F. Persons	Richmond County 28 Jan 1854
Ignatius Fleming	23	Columbia County	Born in Georgia	Floyd Thomas	Carpenter Richmond County
Jane Collins, his wife	24	Richmond County	Born in Georgia	Floyd Thomas	Seamstress Richmond County
& two children, John	8	Richmond County	Born in Georgia	Floyd Thomas	Richmond County
& William		Richmond County	Born in Georgia	Floyd Thomas	Richmond County
Nancy Coleman	28	South Carolina	1834	L. L. Antony	Richmond County 4 Apr 1854
William Byrd	16	Richmond County	Born in Richmond	Allen King	Laborer Richmond

Name	Age	Nativity	Time of Coming to Georgia	Guardian	Occupation, Residence, and Date of Registration
			County		County
Stephen Coleman	33	South Carolina	Arrived 1846	Gary F. Parish	Painter in Augusta since 1846 20 Apr 1854
Barbary Coleman	31	South Carolina	Arrived 1839	Gary F. Parish	Seamstress in Augusta since 1839 20 Apr 1854
Mary Harman	30	South Carolina	Arrived 1847	Tho[s] J. Calvin	Seamstress in Augusta since 1848 22 Apr 1854
Vienna Carnes	50	Richmond County		James Harper	Washer & ironer 27 Apr 1854
Sarah Carnes	27	Richmond County		James Harper	Seamstress 27 Apr 1854
Simuel Carnes	19	Richmond County		James Harper	Drayman 27 Apr 1854
Isiah Carnes	16	Richmond County		James Harper	Drayman 27 Apr 1854
Mathew Carnes	11	Richmond County		James Harper	Drayman 27 Apr 1854
Judy Parks	19	Burke County		Allen C. Harbin	Washer & ironer Richmond County 1853 1 May 1854
James Parks	23	Richmond County		Allen C. Harbin	Drayman Richmond County 1 May 1854

Name	Age	Nativity	Time of Coming to Georgia	Guardian	Occupation, Residence, and Date of Registration
Precilla Kelly	16	Richmond County		John Nelson	Seamstress Richmond County 2 May 1854
Mary Hoxie	34	Wilkes County		Charles Catlin	Seamstress Richmond County 8 Jun 1854
Emma Hoxie	8	Richmond County		Charles Catlin	Richmond County 8 Jun 1854
Augustus		Richmond County		Charles Catlin	Richmond County 8 Jun 1854
Mary Jane		Richmond County		Charles Catlin	Richmond County 8 Jun 1854
& two young children of Mary Hoxie		Richmond County		Charles Catlin	Richmond County 8 Jun 1854
William Hoxie	22	Wilkes County		Charles Catlin	Richmond County 8 Jun 1854
Jane Moore	29	South Carolina	Arrived 1847	Gary F. Parish	Richmond County 10 Jun 1854
Phillis Russell	60	Georgia	Arrived 1839	James Harper	Common laborer Richmond County 12 Jun 1854
Abiah Russell	25	Georgia	Arrived 1839	James Harper	House servant Richmond County

Name	Age	Nativity	Time of Coming to Georgia	Guardian	Occupation, Residence, and Date of Registration
					12 Jun 1854
Morris Russell	26	Georgia	Arrived 1839	James Harper	Common laborer Richmond County 12 Jun 1854
Elizabeth Collins	18	Georgia	Arrived 1848	E. C. Tinsley	Seamstress Richmond County 12 Jun 1854
Edmond Youngblood	28	South Carolina	Arrived 1832	G. F. Parish	Bricklayer Richmond County 3 Jul 1854
Jordan Scott	32	South Carolina	Arrived 1840	G. F. Parish	Drayman Richmond County 1840 3 Jul 1854
Anderson Youngblood	26	South Carolina		A. G. Miller	Drayman Richmond County 31 Jul 1854
Melville Lyons	19	Georgia		Sam[l] H. Crump	Bricklayer Richmond County 31 Aug 1854
Festus Lyons	20	Georgia		Sam[l] H. Crump	Bricklayer Richmond County 31 Aug 1854
Elbert Lyons	22	Georgia		Sam[l] H. Crump	Bricklayer Richmond County 31 Aug 1854

Name	Age	Nativity	Time of Coming to Georgia	Guardian	Occupation, Residence, and Date of Registration
Martha Kelly	36	Georgia		G. F. Parish	Washer & ironer Richmond County 31 Aug 1854
Quilley Youngblood	40	South Carolina	Arrived 1824	G. F. Parish	Washer & ironer Richmond County 31 Aug 1854
Augustus Youngblood	20	Georgia		G. F. Parish	Laborer Richmond County 31 Aug 1854
Sarah Jane Youngblood	15	Georgia		G. F. Parish	House servant Richmond County 31 Aug 1854
Hannah Todd	50	Georgia		L. L. Antony	Washer & ironer Richmond County 31 Aug 1854
Nancy Coleman	29	South Carolina	Arrived 1834	L. L.. Antony	Seamstress Richmond County 1846 23 May 1855
Mary Harman	31	South Carolina	Arrived 1847	Tho⁵ J. Calvin	Seamstress Richmond County 1848 28 May 1855
Maria Harman	5				Seamstress 28 May 1855
Barbary Harman	3				Seamstress 28 May 1855

Name	Age	Nativity	Time of Coming to Georgia	Guardian	Occupation, Residence, and Date of Registration
Virginia Harman	1				Seamstress 28 May 1855
Leonora Violeau	30	Augusta			Seamstress 2 Jun 1855
George Violeau	14				
Frances Gardiner	15			S. C. Grenville	Seamstress 11 Jun 1855
Cyrus Brister	21				

Returns for 1855 & 1857

The clerk entered Augusta as the residence for all of the registrants.

Name	Age	Nativity	Time of Coming to Georgia	Guardian	Occupation
Frances Gardner	16	Augusta	Born	F. C. Barber	Seamstress
Fanny Gardner	46	Savannah	1834	F. C. Barber	Seamstress
Amanda Gant	24	Augusta	1834	J. K. Kilburn	Seamstress
Joseph T. Gant	3	Augusta	1834	J. K. Kilburn	Seamstress
Sarah Dent	17	Augusta		James Harper	Nurse
Nancy Coleman	39	Richmond County	1826	L. L. Antony	Seamstress
Mary Harman	32	South Carolina	Arrived 1847	Thos J. Calvin	Seamstress
Julia Green	35	Augusta	Arrived 1847	E. A. Wagnon	Nurse
George Green	15	Augusta	Arrived 1847	E. A. Wagnon	Nurse
Stephen Coleman	36	South Carolina	1846	G. F. Parish	Painter
Nancy Coleman	31	Richmond County	1826	L. L. Antony	Seamstress Registered 22 Jun 1857
William Corbin	35	Columbia County	Born	Thos Wylds	Farmer Registered 1857

Returns for 1858

The original table has no column headings, but appear to contain the same information as previous lists. The clerk entered Augusta as the residence for all of the registrants, with a few exceptions that are noted.

Name	Age	Nativity	Time of Coming to Georgia	Guardian	Occupation
Eliza Turner	26	Richmond County	Augusta	J. B. Johnson, Temporary Guardian	Laundress Residence lately in Atlanta
Lucy Ruff & four children	25	Warren County	Warren County	T. J. Calvin	Laundress Residence lately in Warrenton
Henry		Warren County	Warren County	T. J. Calvin	Laundress Residence lately in Warrenton
Harrison		Warren County	Warren County	T. J. Calvin	Laundress Residence lately in Warrenton
Noah		Warren County	Warren County	T. J. Calvin	Laundress Residence lately in Warrenton
James		Warren County	Warren County	T. J. Calvin	Laundress Residence lately in Warrenton
Jane Moore	33	South Carolina	South Carolina	N. A. Ford	Seamstress
Leonora Davis	35	Augusta	Augusta	N. A. Ford	Nurse
Emily Kelly (Benefield)	40	Augusta	Augusta	N. A. Ford	Seamstress
John Kelly	21	Augusta	Augusta	N. A. Ford	Tailor
Victoria Ruff	17	Augusta	Augusta	N. A. Ford	Laundress

Laura Kelly	30	Augusta	Augusta	J. A. Christian	Laundress
Thomas Kelly	20	Augusta	Augusta	H. D. Bell	Blacksmith
Lloyd Hoxie	15	Augusta	Augusta	W. D. Leonard	Barber
Barbary Coleman	35	South Carolina	Augusta	W. M. Hight	Seamstress
Affus Hill (C)	30	Augusta	Augusta	B. H. Warren	Laundress
Diana Key (C)	33	Augusta	Augusta	B. H. Warren	Laundress
Jane Johnson	33	Richmond County	Augusta	N. A. Ford	Seamstress
Louisa Scott	18	Richmond County	Augusta	N. A. Ford	Cook
Ann Kelly	44	Augusta	Augusta	James Gardner	Washer & ironer
William Kelly	24	Augusta	Augusta	James Gardner	Barber
Ann Eliza Kelly & child 10 months old	22	Augusta	Augusta	James Gardner	Laundress
Martha Johnson	23	Augusta	Augusta	N. A. Ford	Laundress
Mary Hoxie & her children	38	Washington	Born	W. H. Wheeler	laundress
Mary Jane	8	Augusta	Born	W. H. Wheeler	
Alonzo	7	Augusta	Born	W. H. Wheeler	
Mildred	4	Augusta	Born	W. H. Wheeler	

Wm Henry	6 mos	Augusta	Born	W. H. Wheeler	
Augustus	13	Augusta	Born	W. H. Wheeler	
Frances Hoxie & children, Miflin & Mary	57	Augusta	Born	W. H. Wheeler	Seamstress
Josephine Hoxie	19	Augusta	Born	U. L. Leonard	Nurse
Corinthe Hoxie	16	Augusta	Born	U. L. Leonard	Seamstress
Peter Johnson	56	Augusta	Born	B. F. Hall	Blacksmith
Sarah Johnson & her children, Billy, Susannah, Mary, & Nancy Ann	56	Augusta	Born	B. F. Hall	Laundress
Henry Johnson	19	Augusta	Born	B. F. Hall	Blacksmith
David Johnson	17	Augusta	Born	B. F. Hall	Blacksmith
John Johnson	18	Augusta	Born	B. F. Hall	Blacksmith
Peter Johnson	22	Augusta	Born	B. F. Hall	Blacksmith
John Kelly	26	Augusta	Born	B. F. Hall	Barber
Hannah Todd	58	Augusta	Born	L. Antony	Laundress
Margaret Pleasant & three children	23	Augusta	Born	B. F. Hall	Seamstress
Sarah Eliza Pleasant	6	Augusta	Born	B. F. Hall	
Mary Frances Pleasant	4	Augusta	Born	B. F. Hall	
Madison	10	Augusta	Born	B. F. Hall	

Pleasant	mos				
Susan Todd	44	Augusta	Born	Jonathan Miller	Seamstress
Dianna Ruff	36	Columbia County	Born	Jnº A. Christian	Seamstress
James Newton Ruff	15	Columbia County	Born	Jnº A. Christian	Harness maker
Rushell Brister	52	Augusta	Born	Jn Phinizy	Laundress
Adaline Parker	30	South Carolina	Born	J. W. Whitlock	Cook
Vienna Carnes	54	Augusta	Born	Jaˢ Harper	Laundress
Sarah Carnes	31	Augusta	Born	Jaˢ Harper	Laudress
Isiah Carnes	20	Augusta	Born	Jaˢ Harper	Drayman
Mathew Carnes	15	Augusta	Born	Jaˢ Harper	Drayman
Simuel Carnes	23	Augusta	Born	Jaˢ Harper	Drayman
James Williams	40	Augusta	Born	N. A. Ford	Store servant
Frances Gardner & child 7 months old	19	Augusta	Born	F. C. Barber	seamstress
Amanda Gantt	27	Augusta	Born	Juslaus A. Sneed	Seamstress
James Parks	27	Augusta	Born	E. J. Walker	Drayman
Judy Parks	23	Burke County	1853	A. C. Harbin	Laundress
Stephen Coleman	39	South Carolina	1846	Geº Parish	Painter
Priscilla Kelly	20	Richmond County	1853	B. C. Dinnick	Seamstress
Frances Scott	14	Richmond	Born	N. A. Ford	Cook

		County			
Frances Marmont	30	Columbia	1848	C. Smalley	Laundress
Barton & Ann, her children		Columbia		C. Smalley	
Mary Ruff	31	Warren County	1853	J. A. Christian	Seamstress
& Diana, her daughter	11	Warren County		J. A. Christian	
Martha M. King	21	Burke County		J. A. Christian	Wash & ironer
Martha Kelly	40	Augusta		Saml H. Crump	Laundress
Cornelia Youngblood	23	South Carolina	1853	Ge^o Parish	Laundress
Aug. Youngblood	24	Augusta		Ge^o Parish	Laundress
Pompey Youngblood	27	South Carolina	An infant	Ge^o Parish	Brick mason
Matilda Youngblood	23	South Carolina	An infant	Ge^o Parish	Washer
Joshua Youngblood	21	South Carolina	An infant	Ge^o Parish	Boatman
Quilley Youngblood	44	South Carolina	An infant	Ge^o Parish	Laundress
Jordan Scott	36	South Carolina	An infant	Ge^o Parish	Drayman
Larey King	23	Georgia	An infant	Wm E. Barnes	Laundress
Her brother Jesse	14	Georgia	An infant	Wm E. Barnes	Laundress

Her mother Patsey	60	Georgia	An infant	Wm E. Barnes	Laundress
Ellen Clark	36	Georgia	An infant	W. B. Savage	Cook
Daniel Narius	19	Georgia	An infant	W. B. Savage	Farmer
Emily Brister	23	Georgia	An infant	Jno Phinizy, J^r	washerwoman
Ann Scott	40	Georgia	An infant	N. A. Ford	Washerwoman
Sarah Commander	19	Georgia	An infant		
Darkis Youngblood	23	Georgia	An infant	James Halbert	Washerwoman
Caroline Youngblood & son, Frank, aged 2	25	Georgia	An infant	James Halbert	Washerwoman
Malinda Johnson	32	Georgia	An infant	D. B. Thompson	Seamstress
Maria Ruff	45	Georgia	An infant	T. J. Calvin	
Royall Lett	30	Georgia	An infant	L. C. Mastin	
Henry Lett	20	Georgia	An infant	W. R. McLaws	
Martha Lett & child	47	Georgia	An infant	W. R. McLaws	
Virginia Sibbald	19			S. H. Crump	
& infant Amelia	9 mos				.
Jane Sibbald	48	Georgia	An infant	S. H. Crump	Laundress
& her children, Joseph	14	Georgia	An infant	S. H. Crump	

Emma Louise	14	Georgia	An infant	S. H. Crump	
Mary Jane Sibbald	15	Georgia	An infant	S. H. Crump	
David Sibbald	17	Georgia	An infant	S. H. Crump	
Charles Sibbald	21	Georgia	An infant	S. H. Crump	Blacksmith
Milly Sibbald	20	Georgia	An infant	S. H. Crump	Laundress
Louisa Sibbald & her children	33	Georgia	An infant	S. H. Crump	Laundress
William	13	Georgia	An infant	S. H. Crump	Laundress
Elizabeth	8	Georgia	An infant	S. H. Crump	Laundress
Eugene	6	Georgia	An infant	S. H. Crump	Laundress
Ellen Sibbald	15	Georgia	An infant	S. H. Crump	Laundress
Edward Sibbald	20	Georgia	An infant	S. H. Crump	Barber
Jane Sibbald	18	Georgia	An infant	S. H. Crump	Brick mason
Sarah J. Youngblood	19	Georgia	An infant	G. Parish	House servant
& child Mary Malinda	11 mos	Georgia	An infant	G. Parish	
Jane Youngblood	30	South Carolina	An infant	Dr H. Brignon	Wash & ironer
Ann Youngblood	28	South Carolina	An infant	N. R. Butler	Wash & ironer
Anderson Youngblood	34	South Carolina	An infant	W. P. Lawson	Laborer
Patsey Scott	19	South Carolina	An infant	G. A. Brandon	Washerwoman
Mary Gantt & her children	32	Augusta	An infant	Jno D. Smith	Seamstress

Jane		Augusta	An infant	Jn[o] D. Smith	
Adolphus	11	Augusta	An infant	Jn[o] D. Smith	
Henry	8	Augusta	An infant	Jn[o] D. Smith	
Margaret Kelly & her children	31	Augusta	An infant	H. A. Brignon, Temporary	Cook
Olivia	13	Augusta	An infant	H. A. Brignon, Temporary	
Katy	9	Augusta	An infant	H. A. Brignon, Temporary	
Emily	7	Augusta	An infant	H. A. Brignon, Temporary	
John	5	Augusta	An infant	H. A. Brignon, Temporary	
Anna Margaret	2	Augusta	An infant	H. A. Brignon, Temporary	
An infant child	1	Augusta	An infant	H. A. Brignon, Temporary	
Sarah Kelly	20	Augusta	An infant	H. A. Brignon, Temporary	Seamstress
Thomas Kelly	18	Augusta	An infant	H. A. Brignon, Temporary	
Mary Eliza Kelly	16	Augusta	An infant	H. A. Brignon, Temporary	
Pleasants Brister	30	Savannah	An infant	Jn[o] Phinizy,	Laundress

& children				J^r	
Lydia	8	Savannah	An infant	Jno Phinizy, J^r	
Tench	6	Savannah	An infant	Jno Phinizy, J^r	
Henry Brister	16	Savannah	An infant	Jno Phinizy, J^r	Drayman
Jeff Collins	38	Augusta	An infant	S. H. Oliver	Drayman
Elizabeth Collins, wife	22	Burke County	1848	E. C. Tinsley	Seamstress
Robert A. Harper	35	Augusta	Born	F. H. Miller	Piano tuner
Mary Williams & daughter	27	Burke County	1844	A. Wilson	Seamstress
Ann Eliza	13	Richmond County	Born	A. Wilson	Seamstress
Lucy Carnes & her children	59	South Carolina	An infant	H. D. Bell	Seamstress
Sarah Williams	30	South Carolina	An infant	H. D. Bell	Seamstress
Elizabeth Williams	32	South Carolina	An infant	H. D. Bell	Seamstress
Francis Williams	35	South Carolina	An infant	H. D. Bell	Drayman
Julus Carnes	19	Augusta	Born	B. H. Wasden	Drayman
William Lett	38			W. P. Lawson	Blacksmith
Betsy Keating	45			N. A. Ford	Seamstress
Mary Harman & her children	35	South Carolina		T. J. Calvin	Seamstress

Maria	10	South Carolina		T. J. Calvin	
Barbara	8	South Carolina		T. J. Calvin	
Virginia	5	South Carolina		T. J. Calvin	
Letitia N. Kent	37	South Carolina	1852	J. E. McMurphy	Seamstress
Priscilla Griffin & her children	30	Richmond County	Born	T. W. Miller	Seamstress
Jame	13	Richmond County	Born	T. W. Miller	
Louisa	11	Richmond County	Born	T. W. Miller	
Virginia	9	Richmond County	Born	T. W. Miller	
Mary Ann	7	Richmond County	Born	T. W. Miller	
Milly Ann	5	Richmond County	Born	T. W. Miller	
Robert Griffin	26	Richmond County	Born	T. W. Miller	Laborer
Samuel Burnett	55	Warrenton	Born	R. D. Glover	Laborer
Rebecca Jane Burnett	48	Warrenton	Born	R. D. Glover	Washerwoman
Elixena	16	Warrenton	Born	R. D. Glover	
Loidane	8	Warrenton	Born	R. D. Glover	
Martha Kelly	33	Augusta	Born	W. Lawson	Seamstress Residence

					Savannah
Richmond Lett	35	Augusta	Born	Foster Blodgett	Blacksmith
Eliza Lett	27	Augusta	Born	Foster Blodgett	Seamstress
Jordan Valentine	36	Taliaferro County	June 1858	Mark E. Swinney	Laborer
William Lett	39	Augusta		W. P. Lawson	Blacksmith

Returns for August 1859

Name	Age	Nativity	Time of Coming to Georgia	Guardian	Occupation
Jane Johnson	34	Augusta		N. A. Ford	Seamstress
Betsey Keating	46	Augusta		N. A. Ford	Seamstress
Frances Scott	15	Augusta		N. A. Ford	Seamstress
Laura Scott	19	Augusta		N. A. Ford	Seamstress
James Williams	41	Augusta		N. A. Ford	Store servant
Eliza Turner	26	Augusta		N. A. Ford	Laundress
Frances Hoxie	59	Columbia County	1832	U. L. Leonard	Seamstress
Josephine Hoxie	20	Augusta	Born	U. L. Leonard	Seamstress
Corinthe Hoxie	17	Augusta	Born	U. L. Leonard	
Miflin Hoxie	13	Augusta	Born	U. L. Leonard	
Mary Hoxie (Little)	6	Augusta	Born	U. L. Leonard	
Mary Hoxie Dick Lamback & children	30	Washington	Born	W. H. Wheeler	Laundress
Augustus	14	Augusta	Born	W. H. Wheeler	
Emma	13	Augusta	Born	W. H. Wheeler	
Mary Jane	9	Augusta	Born	W. H. Wheeler	
Alonzo	6	Augusta	Born	W. H.	

Name	Age	Nativity	Time of Coming to Georgia	Guardian	Occupation
				Wheeler	
Mildred	5	Augusta	Born	W. H. Wheeler	
Wm Henry	18	Md, Augusta	Born	W. H. Wheeler	
Joshua Youngblood	22	Augusta	An infant	Ge^o Parish	Blacksmith
Augustus Youngblood	25	Augusta	Born	D. H. Denning	Laborer
Pompey Youngblood	28	Augusta	Born	D. H. Denning	Laborer
Susan Todd	45	Augusta	Born	Jno M. Miller	Seamstress
Mathew Kelly	41	Augusta	Born	S. H. Crump	Laundress
Abiah Russell	30	Georgia	1839	Ja^s Harper	House servant
Mary Williams	24	South Carolina	1844	A. Wilson	Seamstress
& daughter Ann Eliza	14	Augusta	Born	A. Wilson	
Caroline Youngblood	26	Augusta	Born	Ja^s Hulbert	Laundress
& her son Frank	3	Augusta	Born	Ja^s Hulbert	
Darkis Youngblood	24	Augusta	Born	Ja^s Hulbert	Laundress
Leonora Violeau	45	Augusta	Born	Sam H. Crump	Nurse
Morris Russell	31	Georgia	1839	James Harper	Laborer

Name	Age	Nativity	Time of Coming to Georgia	Guardian	Occupation
Jeff Collins	37	Georgia	Born	S. H. Oliver	Drayman
Elizabeth Collins, his wife	23	Georgia	Born	E. C. Tinsley	Seamstress
Dianna Ruff	38	Warren County	1855	J. A. Christian	Laundress
James Newton, her son	16	Columbia County	1855	J. A. Christian	Harness maker
Lucy Ruff	35	Warren County	1856	N. K. Boutter	Laundress
Mary Ann Ruff	32	Warren County	1854	J. A. Christian	Seamstress
Dianna, her daughter	12	Warren County	1854	J. A. Christian	
Samuel Burnett	54	Warren County		R. D. Glover	Laborer
Rebecca Jane Burnett	50	Warren County		R. D. Glover	Laundress
Elexina Burnett	17	Warren County		R. D. Glover	Laundress
Loidane Burnett	7	Warren County		R. D. Glover	Laundress
Lavey King	25	Richmond County		W. E. Barnes	Laundress
Patsey, her son	15	Richmond County		W. E. Barnes	Laundress
Jesse	15	Richmond County		W. E. Barnes	Laundress
Martha King	22	Richmond County		W. E. Barnes	Laundress

Name	Age	Nativity	Time of Coming to Georgia	Guardian	Occupation
Lizzie Dent	28	Augusta		W. P. Lawson	Laundress
Hannah Todd	49	Augusta		D. L. Anthony	Laundress
Ellen Clark	37	Augusta	Born	W. B. Savage	Cook
Daniel Narius, her son	20	Augusta	Born	W. B. Savage	Farmer
Thos Dent	28	Augusta		Ja^s Harper	Painter
Sarah Commander	20	Augusta	Born	E. C. Tinsley	Laundress
Malinda Johnson	33	Augusta		D. B. Thomson, Guard	Seamstress
Adaline Parker	31	South Carolina	At 10 years of age	J. A. Whitlock	Cook
W. Henry Barefield	22	Augusta		S. H. Crump	Carpenter
Caroline Valentine	26	Warren County	To Augusta 1851	N. A. Ford	Laundress
Sarah J. Youngblood	20	Richmond County	Born	R. H. Coker	Laundress
Peter Johnson, Senr	58	Augusta	Born	B. J. Hall	Blacksmith
Sarah Johnson, his wife	58	Augusta	Born	B. J. Hall	
Billy Johnson, his son	<14	Augusta	Born	B. J. Hall	
Susannah Johnson, his	<14	Augusta	Born	B. J. Hall	

Name	Age	Nativity	Time of Coming to Georgia	Guardian	Occupation
daughter					
Nancy Ann, his daughter	<14	Augusta	Born	B. J. Hall	
Peter Johnson, Junr	23	Augusta	Born	B. J. Hall	Blacksmith
Henry Johnson	20	Augusta	Born	B. J. Hall	
John Johnson	19	Augusta	Born	B. J. Hall	
David Johnson	18	Augusta	Born	B. J. Hall	
Farriby Jane Burnett	17	Warren County	1859	Joshua Butt	House servant
Laura Kelly	31	Augusta	Augusta	J. A. Chritian	Laundress
Cornelia Kelly	24	South Carolina		D. K. Denning	Laundress
Margaret Pleasants & her children	24	Augusta		B. F. Hall	Laundress
Sarah Eliza	6	Augusta		B. F. Hall	
Mary Francis	5	Augusta		B. F. Hall	
Madison	2	Augusta		B. F. Hall	
Martha Ann, infant		Augusta		B. F. Hall	
Jordan Scott				J. H. Oliver	
Aquilla Youngblood				J. H. Oliver	
Sarah Williams	31	Augusta	An infant	H. D. Bell	Laundress

Name	Age	Nativity	Time of Coming to Georgia	Guardian	Occupation
Catharine Bugg & her children	24	Augusta	An infant	Cha[s] Catlin	laundress
W Thomas	7	Augusta		Cha Catlin	
Eliza	5	Augusta		Cha[s] Catlin	
Maria	2	Augusta		Cha Catlin	
Charles Ladivez	21	Augusta		L. A. Dugas	Cabinet maker
Mary Jane Ladivez & her children	26	Augusta		L. A. Dugas	
John	5	Augusta		L. A. Dugas	
Robert	4	Augusta		L. A. Dugas	
Josephine	3	Augusta		L. A. Dugas	
Robert Harper	36	Augusta		F. H. Miller	Piano tuner
Laura Harper & their children	30	Augusta		F. H. Miller	Seamstress
Thomas	10	Augusta		F. H. Miller	
Robert	8	Augusta		F. H. Miller	
James	6	Augusta		F. H. Miller	
Martha	4	Augusta		F. H. Miller	
Samuel	18 mos	Augusta		F. H. Miller	
Martha Beall	40	Augusta		F. H. Miller	Seamstress
Mary Banyer	69	Augusta		L. A. Dugas	Seamstress
Eliza Johnson	54	Augusta		F. Blodgett	Seamstress

Name	Age	Nativity	Time of Coming to Georgia	Guardian	Occupation
Viena Carnes & her son	56	Augusta		James Harper	Laundress
Mathew Carnes	16	Augusta		James Harper	Drayman
Josiah Carnes	21	Augusta		James Harper	Drayman
Simuel Carnes	24	Augusta		James Harper	Drayman
Mary Gant	33	Augusta		J. D. Smith	Seamstress
Jane Gant	8	Augusta		J. D. Smith	Seamstress
Adolphus Gant	11	Augusta		J. D. Smith	Seamstress
Henry Gant	9	Augusta		J. D. Smith	Seamstress
Ann Kelly	45	Augusta		James Gardner	Laundress
Ann Eliza Kelly	24	Augusta		James Gardner	Laundress
Henry Raymond Kelly	25	Augusta		James Gardner	Barber
Cheney King	30	Augusta		W. E. Barnes	Laundress
Virginia Sibbald	20	Augusta		S. H. Crump	
James Sibbald	19	Augusta		S. H. Crump	
Ellen Sibbald	16	Augusta		S. H. Crump	
Edward Sibbald	21	Augusta		S. H. Crump	
Milly Sibbald	29	Augusta		S. H. Crump	
Louisa Sibbald	33	Augusta		S. H. Crump	

Name	Age	Nativity	Time of Coming to Georgia	Guardian	Occupation
& her children					
William	14	Augusta		S. H. Crump	
Elizabeth	9	Augusta		S. H. Crump	
Eugene	7			S. H. Crump	
Jane Sibbald	49			S. H. Crump	
Joseph	15			S. H. Crump	
Emma	14			S. H. Crump	
Louisa	14			S. H. Crump	
Mary Jane	15			S. H. Crump	

Returns for August 1860

The original list has no column headings, but appears to contain much of the same information as previous lists.

Name	Age	Nativity	Complexion	Occupation	Guardian
Gideon Jones	22	Warren County			T. J. Calvin, Temporary Guardian
Sarah Ruff & children		Taliaferro County			Joshua O'Neil
Dilsey					
Maria					
Harrison					
Laura					
Vincent					
Susan Todd	45		Black	Seamstress	J. M. Miller
Diana Key	35		Black	Baker	Ge W. Lamar
Diana Ruff	39		Black	Laundress	J. A. Christian
James Newton, her son	17		Brown	Harness maker	J. A. Christian
Lucy Ruff	35		Mulatto	Laundress	N. R. Buttler
Henry Ruff	15		Mulatto	Blacksmith	N. R. Buttler
Harrison Ruff	12		Mulatto	Farmer	N. R. Buttler
Noah Ruff	8		Brown		N. R. Buttler
Jonas Ruff	6		Brown		N. R. Buttler
John Carnes	18		Black	Drayman	Ge° W. Lamar
Nora Davis	35		Mulatto	Nurse	S. H. Crump

Name	Age	Nativity	Complexion	Occupation	Guardian
Sarah Williams	32		Brown	Laundress	H. D. Bell
Charles Ladivez	30		Mulatto	Cabinet maker	L. A. Dugas
Mary Janes Ladivez & their children	27		Mulatto	Laundress	L. A. Dugas
John	5		Mulatto		L. A. Dugas
Robert	4		Mulatto		L. A. Dugas
Josephine	3		Mulatto		L. A. Dugas
Matilda, infant			Mulatto		L. A. Dugas
Isabella Moore	71				J. Phinizy, Sen
Martha King	23		Brown	Laundress	W. E. Barnes
Laney King	26		Brown	Laundress	W. E. Barnes
Sarah Commander			Mulatto	Laundress	E. C. Tinsley
Martha Kelly	41		Brown	Laundress	S. H. Crump
Priscilla Kelly	22		Black	Laundress	J. Nelson
Jordon Valentine	37		Black	Drayman	M. E. Swinney
Caroline Valentine	27		Black	Laundress	M. E. Swinney
Mary Rebecca Valentine		Born 1852	Black		M. E. Swinney
Laura M. Valentine		Born 1854	Black		M. E. Swinney
William B. Valentine		Born 1856	Black		M. E. Swinney
Samuel		Born 1859	Black		M. E. Swinney

Name	Age	Nativity	Complexion	Occupation	Guardian
Valentine					
Caroline Johnson	55		Black	Seamstress	F. Blodget
Abiah Russell	31		Black	Laundress	Ja Harper
Lizzie Dent	29		Yellow	Laundress	W. P. Lawson
Mary Ann Ruff	33		Black	Seamstress	J. A. Christian
Diana, her daughter	12		Black		J. A. Christian
Jane Johnson	34		Black	Seamstress	N. A. Ford
Laura Scott	20		Mulatto	Seamstress	N. A. Ford
Catharine Bugg & her children	25		Mulatto	Seamstress	L. L. Catlin
Thomas	8		Mulatto		L. L. Catlin
Eliza	6		Mulatto		L. L. Catlin
Maria Martha	3				L. L. Catlin
Sarah	8 mos				L. L. Catlin
Milly Sibbald	30		Brown	Seamstress	S. H. Crump
Louisa Sibbald	15		Brown	Seamstress	S. H. Crump
Ellen Sibbald	17		Brown	Seamstress	S. H. Crump
Mary Jane Sibbald	16		Brown	Seamstress	S. H. Crump
Virginia Sibbald	21		Brown	Seamstress	S. H. Crump
David Sibbald	15		Brown	Seamstress	S. H. Crump
Betsey Keating (Ford)	46		Brown	Seamstress	N. A. Ford

Returns for 1861

The original list has no column headings, but appears to contain much of the same information as previous lists.

Name	Age	Nativity	Complexion	Occupation	Guardian
David Scott	50	South Carolina		Farm hand	Arch Cadle
Thomas Singleton, alias Black	18	Augusta			J. C. Snead
Adaline Scott	24	Augusta			Joseph Graham
William Benning	40	Columbia	Black	Laborer	E. Hicks
Frances Benning	40	Columbia	Black		E. Hicks
Simon Benning	14	Columbia	Black		E. Hicks
Hensley Benning	19	Columbia	Black	Blacksmith	Jnº A. Bahler
Elizabeth Senks	20	Columbia	Black	Laundress	Jnº A. Bahler
Augustus Senks	4	Columbia	Black	Laundress	Jnº A. Bahler
Joanna Senks	3	Columbia	Black	Laundress	Jnº A. Bahler
Jim Benning	16	Columbia	Black	Carpenter	Jnº A. Bahler
Dianna Ruff	40	Warren County	Black	Laundress	Jnº A. Christian
James Newton, her son	18	Columbia County	Black	Harness maker	Jnº A. Christian
Mary Ann Ruff	34	Warren County	Black	Seamstress	Jnº A. Christian
Dianna Ruff, her daughter	13	Warren County	Black	Seamstress	Jnº A. Christian

Name	Age	Nativity	Complexion	Occupation	Guardian
William Harman	24	Richmond County	Mulatto	Brick mason	A. W. Rhodes, Temp
Ned Kelly	39	Richmond County	Black	Laborer	Alex Deas
Abiah Russell	32	Georgia	Black	House servant	Ja^s Harper
Palmer Grubbs	22	Georgia	Brown	Seamstress	G. A. Snead
Abiah Russell	32	Georgia	Black	House servant	Albert Webster
Sarah Ann Chisholm	20	Georgia	Brown	Laundress	G. A. Snead
John Harman	24	Georgia	Yellow	Brick mason	Edwd Tabb
James Valentine	35	Georgia	Black	Drayman	Albert Webster

Court of Ordinary 1863 to ___

The clerk entered Richmond County as the residence for all of the registrants, that is not repeated here.

Name	Age	Parentage	Nativity	Occupation	Description
Patsey King	68	Cheney King	Greene County	Nurse	Brown
Cheney King	37	Patsey King	Greene County	Cook, washer, & ironer	Brown
Lovey King	28	Patsey King	Troup County	Cook, washer, & ironer	Brown
Edward Lee King	17	Cheney King	Troup County	Laborer	Brown
Robert A. Harper	41	Polly Keating	Augusta	Piano Turner	Mulatto
Martha Kelly	42	Juno Kelly	Augusta	Washer & ironer	Brown
Jane Johnson	37	Nancy Johnson	Augusta	Seamstress	Mulatto
Laura Scott	23	Ann Scott	Augusta	Seamstress	Mulatto
Priscilla Griffin	36	Pheriby Griffin	Richmond County	Seamstress	Mulatto
James Griffin	16	Priscilla Griffin	Richmond County	Farmer	Dark
Daniel Scott	52	Patsey Scott	South Carolina	Carpenter	Dark
Martha King	26	Patsey King	Troup County	Laundress	Dark
Mary Williams	32	Hannah Reynolds	South Carolina	Seamstress	Mulatto
Robert Green	14	Sarah Green	Augusta	Laborer	Brown
Amelia Moore	39		South Carolina	Seamstress	Brown

136

Name	Age	Parentage	Nativity	Occupation	Description
Frank Williams	40	Lucy Williams	Augusta	Drayman	Brown
Lucy Low	40	Hannah Parks	Greene County	Seamstress	Brown
Darkis Youngblood	28	Rebecca Youngblood	South Carolina	Washer & ironer	Mulatto
Samuel Burnett	58	Jane Burnett	Warren County	Drayman	Brown
Rebecca Jane Burnett	54	Jane Moats	Columbia County	Seamstress	Mulatto
Elexina Burnett	16	Rebecca Jane Burnett	Warren County	Seamstress	Brown
Mary Hoxie	43	Frances Hoxie	Washington County	Seamstress	Mulatto
Matilda Bowers	51	Mary Kelly	South Carolina	Nurse	Mulatto
Julia Kelly	24	Emily Kelly	Augusta	Seamstress	Mulatto
Diana Ruff	40	Fanny Ruff	Warren County	Washer & ironer	Black
Leonora Violeau	49	Jane Violeau	Augusta	Nurse	Mulatto
Priscilla Kelly	30	Mary Kelly	South Carolina	Seamstress	Mulatto
Emily Kelly	45	Judy Kelly	Augusta	Seamstress	Black
Eliza Johnson	58	Priscilla Johnson	Augusta	Seamstress	Brown
Ellen Clark	41	Charlotte Scott	Burke County	Tripe seller	Mulatto
Daniel Nurris	24	Ellen Clark	Burke County	Farmer	Mulatto
Lucy Ruff	38	Rachel Ruff	Warren County	Cook	Mulatto
Leonora Kent	30	Rebecca Maxwell	Charleston, South Carolina	Dress maker	Bright mulatto
William Benning	42	Hannah Benning	Columbia County	Farmer	Black

137

Name	Age	Parentage	Nativity	Occupation	Description
Eliza Ann Kelly	28	Ann Kelly	Augusta	Seamstress	Mulatto
John Dent	36	Chloe Dent	Augusta	Blacksmith	Mulatto
Henrietta Dent	41	Chloe Dent	Augusta	Washer & ironer	Mulatto
Chloe Ann Dent	17	Henrietta Dent	Richmond County	Washer & ironer	Black
Joseph Scott	22	Dicey Scott	Richmond County	House servant	Brown
Emma Jane Kelly	23	Betsey Kelly	Augusta	Seamstress	Black
Robert Griffin	41	Pheriby Griffin	Richmond County	Farmer	Mulatto
Elizabeth Dent	35	Myra Dent	Augusta	Seamstress	Mulatto
Elizabeth Seals	25	Rosetta Benning	Columbia County	Washer & ironer	Black
Frances Benning	42	Keziah Mandrow	Columbia County	Seamstress	Black
Jesse King	19	Patsey King	Troup County	Laborer	Black
William Henry Barefield	29	Jane Brux	Augusta	Carpenter	Mulatto
Jane Sibbald	53	Milly Sibbald	Augusta	Washer & ironer	Black
Louisa Sibbald	38	Milly Sibbald	Augusta	Washer & ironer	Black
Milly Sibbald	38	Jane Sibbald	Augusta	Nurse	Black
Virginia Sibbald	27	Jane Sibbald	Augusta	Washer & ironer	Brown
Ned Kelly	41	Jane Kelly	Augusta	Blacksmith	Black

Name	Age	Parentage	Nativity	Occupation	Description
Jeff Collins	43	Polly Collins	Richmond County	Drayman	Mulatto
Henry Ruff	17	Lucy Ruff	Warren County	Blacksmith	Mulatto
Patsey Scott	23	Candis Scott	Greene County	Washer & ironer	Brown
Evelina Fair	46	Phoebe Walker	Augusta	Seamstress	Mulatto
Caroline Scott	30	Eliza Holmes	Charleston, South Carolina	Seamstress	Mulatto
James R. Maxwell	64	Leah Maxwell	Charleston, South Carolina	Carpenter	Mulatto
Jim Benning	18	Rosetta Benning	Columbia County	Laborer	Black
Frances Scott	19	Ann Scott	Augusta	Washer & ironer	Black
Elizabeth Collins	28	Fairee Chavons	Barnwell District, South Carolina	Seamstress	Brown
Thomas Dent	37	Myra Dent	Augusta	Carpenter	Mulatto
John Johnson	23	Sarah Johnson	Augusta	Blacksmith	Mulatto
Fanny Houston	45	Mary Houston	South Carolina	House servant	Mulatto
Frances A. Houston	22	Jane Lewis	South Carolina	Seamstress	Mulatto
Jane Youngblood	36	Jemima Youngblood	Augusta	Washer & ironer	Mulatto
Isabella Moore	73	Nancy Lamar	Richmond County	Seamstress	Mulatto
Affey Hill	35	Rebecca Doctor	Augusta	Laundress	Brown
Harriet Lloyd	61	Jane Lloyd	Savannah	Washer &	Mulatto

Name	Age	Parentage	Nativity	Occupation	Description
				ironer	
Margaret Kelly	52	Betsey Kelly	Augusta	Marketer	Brown
Sarah Kelly	25	Margaret Kelly	Augusta	Seamstress	Mulatto
Lavinia Kelly	17	Margaret Kelly	Augusta	Washer & ironer	Brown
Amanda Gantt	32	Polly Gantt	Augusta	Seamstress	Mulatto
Jordan Scott	49	Nancy Scott	South Carolina	Cotton marker	Mulatto
Aquilla Youngblood	49	Jemima Youngblood	South Carolina	Seamstress	Mulatto
Laura Harper	33	Caroline Bonyer	Augusta	Seamstress	Mulatto
Elizabeth Payne	28	Lucinda Green	Augusta	Seamstress	Mulatto
Mary Eliza Kelly	21	Margaret Kelly	Augusta	Seamstress	Brown
Mary Jane Sibbald	20	Jane Sibbald	Augusta	Nurse	Mulatto
David Sibbald	21	Jane Sibbald	Augusta	Bricklayer	Mulatto
Charles Sibbald	25	Jane Sibbald	Augusta	Blacksmith	Brown
Joseph Sibbald	19	Jane Sibbald	Augusta	Laborer	Mulatto
William Sibbald	18	Louisa Sibbald	Augusta	Varnisher	Black
Ellen Sibbald	20	Louisa Sibbald	Augusta	Nurse	Brown
David Johnson	21	Sarah Johnson	Augusta	Bricklayer	Brown
Betsey Keating	50	Jane Keating	Augusta	Seamstress	Mulatto
Sarah Williams	35	Lucy Williams	Augusta	Washer & ironer	Brown
Susan Todd	54	Peggy Todd	Augusta	Washer &	Black

Name	Age	Parentage	Nativity	Occupation	Description
				ironer	
Thomas Kelly	23	Margaret Kelly	Augusta	Barber	Mulatto
Ann Youngblood	45	Rebecca Youngblood	South Carolina	Washer & ironer	Mulatto
Palmer Grubbs	24	Rebecca Grubbs	South Carolina	House servant	Mulatto
Jane Grubbs	33	Rebecca Grubbs	South Carolina	House servant	Mulatto
William Byrd	24	Keziah Byrd	Richmond County	Farmer	Mulatto
Hensley Benning	22	Rosetta Benning	Columbia County	Blacksmith	Black
Ursula Stith	65	Jane Poisson	North Carolina	Seamstress	Mulatto
Josephine Stith	33	Ursula Stith	Augusta	Seamstress	Mulatto
Martha Beall	44	Jenny Keating	Augusta	Nurse	Mulatto
Edward Sibbald	25	Louisa Sibbald	Augusta	Barber	Black
Charles Ladeveze	33	Caroline Bonyer	Augusta	Cabinet maker	Mulatto
Mary Jane Ladeveze	30	Mary Osmond	Augusta	Dress maker	Mulatto
Peter Johnson	27	Sarah Johnson	Augusta	Blacksmith	Mulatto
William Lett	43	Patsey Lett	Augusta	Blacksmith	Mulatto
Elbert Lyons	31	Anna Lyons	Columbia County	Bricklayer	Mulatto
Sarah Dent	25	Elmira Dent	Augusta	Seamstress	Mulatto
Martha Lett	52	Patsey Lett	Hancock County	Nurse	Mulatto
Joseph Kelly	42	Betsy Kelly	Augusta	Blacksmith	Black

Name	Age	Parentage	Nativity	Occupation	Description
Patsey King	69	Cheney King	Greene County	Seamstress	Brown
Henry Lett	25	Martha Lett	Augusta	Blacksmith	Brown
Vienna Carnes	59	Sarah Carnes	Augusta	Cook	Brown
Sarah Carnes	36	Vienna Carnes	Augusta	Seamstress	Brown
Simuel Carnes	28	Vienna Carnes	Augusta	Drayman	Mulatto
Isaiah Carnes	25	Vienna Carnes	Augusta	Drayman	Mulatto
Mathew Carnes	20	Vienna Carnes	Augusta	Drayman	Mulatto
Royal Lett	35	Patsey Lett	Augusta	Blacksmith	Mulatto
John Carnes	21	Rebecca Doctor	Augusta	Drayman	Black
Diana Key	38	Rebecca Doctor	Augusta	Baker	Black
John Harman	29	Elizabeth Harman	Richmond County	Bricklayer	Yellow
Sarah Ruff	38	Dilsey Ruff	Warren County	Cook	Brown
James Williams	43	Lucy Williams	Augusta	Store steward	Brown
Morris Russell	33	Phillis Russell	Hancock County	Store porter	Brown
Rachel Brister	62	Nannie Telfair	Savannah	Washer	Brown
Victoria Ruff	22	Judy Ruff	Taliaferro County	Washer & ironer	Black
Sarah Jane Youngblood	24	Aquilla Youngblood	Augusta	Washer & ironer	Brown
Cornelia Youngblood	26	Rebecca Youngblood	South Carolina	Washer & ironer	Mulatto
Laura Kelly	36	Judy Kelly	Augusta	Washer & ironer	Brown
Augustus	29	Aquilla	Augusta	Laborer	Brown

Name	Age	Parentage	Nativity	Occupation	Description
Youngblood		Youngblood			
Margaret Pleasants	30	Sarah Johnson	Augusta	Seamstress	Mulatto
Hannah Todd	60	Peggy Todd	Augusta	Cook	Black
Sarah Harris Dent	17	Henrietta Dent	Richmond County	House servant	Mulatto
William Johnson	16	Sarah Johnson	Augusta	Blacksmith	Mulatto
Stephen Coleman	44	Vicy Coleman	South Carolina	Painter	Black
Anderson Youngblood	39	Jemima Youngblood	South Carolina	Carpenter	Mulatto
James Newton Ruff	19	Diana Ruff	Columbia County	Harness maker	Mulatto
Ann Brister	29	Rachel Brister	Augusta	Seamstress	Brown
Mary Harman	40	Barbara Harman	South Carolina	Seamstress	Mulatto
Caroline Youngblood	30	Rebecca Youngblood	South Carolina	Seamstress	Brown
James Parks	30	Betsey Parks	Greene County	Drayman	Black
John Moore	49	Winny Dill	South Carolina	Drayman	Mulatto
Susan Hicks	35	Critta Farm	Columbia County	Seamstress	Mulatto
Louisa Frazier	38	Violet Griffin	Augusta	Tailoress	Mulatto
Richard Lamar	78	Nancy Lamar	Richmond County	Carpenter	Brown
Daniel Lamar	40	Fanny Lamar	Augusta	Carpenter	Brown
Malinda Lamar	36	Fanny Lamar	Augusta	Mantua maker	Mulatto

Name	Age	Parentage	Nativity	Occupation	Description
William A. Lloyd	27	Harriet Lloyd	Augusta	Seamstress	Brown
Mack Parker	35	Ally Parker	Augusta	Washer & ironer	Brown
Aurena Dent	29	Phoeby Burnett	Warren County	Washer & ironer	Mulatto
Chloe Ann Dent	35	Nancy Dent	Augusta	Seamstress	Mulatto
Laura Dent	34	Nancy Dent	Augusta	Washer & ironer	Mulatto
Lovey Ann King	23	Elvira King	Greene County	Washer & ironer	Mulatto
Elizabeth King	40	Patsey King	Greene County	Washer & ironer	Black
John King	17	Elizabeth King	Greene County	Laborer	Brown
Oliver Ruff	24	Fanny Ruff	Warren County	Carpenter	Black
Matilda Kelly	35	Unknown	Augusta	Seamstress	Mulatto
Alice Lamar	37	Rose Cowling	North Carolina	Washer & ironer	Black
Jane Brux	47	Betsy Brux	Augusta	Seamstress	Mulatto
John Barefield	26	Jane Brux	Augusta	Cabinet maker	Mulatto
Emily Barefield	30	Jane Brux	Augusta	Seamstress	Mulatto
Caroline Snowdon	19	Jane Brux	Augusta	Seamstress	Mulatto
Louisa Campbell	22	Jane Brux	Augusta	Seamstress	Mulatto
Lewis Campbell	23	Jane Brux	Augusta	Tinner	Mulatto
Abiah Russell	33	Phillis Russell	Baldwin County	Washer & ironer	Brown

Name	Age	Parentage	Nativity	Occupation	Description
George B. Snowdon	17	Jane Brux	Augusta	Cigar maker	Mulatto
Polly Ann Gantt	40	Betsey Gantt	Columbia County	Washer & ironer	Mulatto
Isaac Harman	71	Elizabeth Harman	Richmond County	Laborer	Mulatto
Betsy Scott	37	Dicey Scott	Columbia County	Washer & ironer	Brown
Aurelia Scott	17	Susan Hicks	Augusta	Seamstress	Lt. mulatto
Caroline Melton	24	Elizabeth Melton	Richmond County	Washer & cook	Mulatto
Martha Sanders	25	Mary Ann Berry	South Carolina	Nurse	Mulatto
Claiborne Turner	21	Becky Edwards	Newton County	Laborer	Black

Fourth Register, 1863

On the cover, the clerk wrote

Free Negro Docket
Court of Ordinary
Richmond County
1863

The pages of the original record volume are not numbered. On the first page, the clerk wrote

Free Negro Docket

Court of Ordinary, Richmond County

The original registrations are in paragraph format, transcribed as follows.

Amelia Moore, 39 years old, born South Carolina, seamstress, brown complexion. Application 25 Apr 1863. Notice given. No objection. Registered May Term 1863 upon oath of Maximillian N. deLettre. Robert M. Phinizy, Guardian.

Lucy Low, 40 years old, born Greene County, seamstress, brown complexion. Application 30 Apr 1863. Notice given. No objection. Registered May Term 1863 upon oath of John B. Carter, Guardian.

Elizabeth Payne, 23 years old, born Augusta, mother Lucinda Green, seamstress, mulatto. Application 13 May 1863. Notice given. No objection. Registered June Term 1863 on oath of William R. Tant and previous certificate.

Fanny Houston, 45 years old, born South Carolina, house servant, mulatto. Application 18 May 1863. Notice given. No objection. Registered June Term 1863 upon oath of Ira D. Mathews, Guardian.

Francis A. Houston, 24 years old, born South Carolina. seamstress, mulatto. Application 18 May 1863. Notice given. No objection. Registered June Term 1863 upon oath of Ira D. Mathews, Guardian.

Herod King, 30 years old, born Troup County, striker for a blacksmith, mother Patsey King, black complexion. Application 20 May 1863. Notice given. Continued June Term. Applicant dead, July Term 1863.

Evelina Fair, 46 years old, born Augusta, seamstress, mulatto, mother Phoebe Walker. Application 20 May 1863. Notice give. No objection. Registered June Term 1863 on oathof Albert Walker, Guardian, & Ira D. Matthews.

Caroline Scott, 30 years old, born Charleston, South Carolina, mother Eliza Holmes, mulatto. Application 21 May 1863. Notice given. No objection. Registered June Term 1863 on oath of Ira D. Matthews, Guardian.

Johnson Smith, 70 years old, born Virginia, mother Lucy Smith, miller & farmer, black complexion. Application 23 May 1863. Notice served on George W. Hall and posted on Court House door. No objection. Registered June Term 1863 on oath of George W. Hall, Guardian.

Emma Jane Kelly, 23 years old, mother Betsy Kelly, born Augusta, seamstress, black complexion. Application 25 May 1863. Notice given. No objection. Registered June Term 1863 upon oath of William R. Tant. Samuel Dunham, Guardian.

James R. Maxwell, 64 years old, mother Leah Maxwell, born Charleston, South Carolina, carpenter, bright mulatto. Application 29 May 1863. Notice given. No objection. Registered June Term 1863 on oath of John E. Marley. John E. Macmurphy, Guardian.

Mary Ann Burnett, 16 years old, mother Amy Burnett, born Warren County, nurse, mulatto. Application 30 May 1863. Notice served on John L. Scott. Continued June Term, July Term, and August Term 1863.

Henry Ruff, 17 years old, mother Lucy Ruff, born Warren County, blacksmith, mulatto. Application 30 May 1863. Notice given. No objection. Registered June term 1863 upon oath of Francis Sanford. Nehemiah K. Poutler, Guardian.

Aurena Dent, 29 years old, Phoebe Burnett, born Warren County, washer & ironer, brown complexion. Notice given to John Bones. Continued June Term 1863. No objection. Registered July Term 1863 upon oath of John A. Bohler. Thomas H. Fisher, Guardian.

Matilda Jones, 20 years old, mother Mary Jones, born Columbia County, washer & ironer, brown complexion. Notice given to Stephen Faughman. Application 30 May 1863. No objection. Registered June Term 1863 upon oath of Gordon Ford. Thomas P. Jones, Guardian.

Joseph Scott, 22 years old, mother Dicey Scott, born Richmond County, house servant, brown complexion. Registered 1 Jun 1863 on oath of Susan Downs and letters of Guardianship produced. Elizabeth Walker, appointed Guardian in 1853 by Inferior Court.

William Griffin, 33 years old, mother Pheriby Griffin, born Richmond County, mulatto, farmer. Application 1 Jun 1863. Notice served on D. B. Hack. Continued July Term and August Term 1863.

Elizabeth King, 40 years old, mother Patsey King, born Greene County, washer & ironer, black complexion. Application 1 Jun 1863. Notice given. No objection. Registered July Term upon oath of Andrew J. Davis. William W. Walker, Guardian.

Aurelia Scott, 17 years old, mother Susan Hicks, born Augusta, seamstress, light mulatto. Application 1 Jun 1863. Notice given. Continued July Term and August Term 1863. Registered September Term 1863 upon oath of Henry Scott.

Oliver Ruff, 24 years old, mother Fanny Ruff, born Warren County, carpenter, black. Application 1 Jun 1863. Notice given. No objection. Registered July Term 1863 upon oath of Martha Holcombe. Erwin Hicks, Guardian.

Louisa Frazier, 38 years old, mother Violet Griffin, born Augusta, tailoress, mulatto. Application 2 Jun 1863. Notice given. No objection. Registered July Term 1863 upon oath of Charles Hall, Guardian.Anton Iversen, Guardian.

William Cleoper, 17 years old, mother Mary Cleoper, born Charleston, South Carolina, laborer, mulatto. Application 2 Jun 1863. Notice given. No objection. Registered July Term 1863 upon oath of Anton Iversen, Guardian.

Susan Hicks, 35 years old, mother Critta Farm, born Columbia County, seamstress, light mulatto. Application 2 Jun 1863. Notice given. No objection. Registered July Term 1863 upon oath of Henry Scott. Archibald B. Crump, Guardian.

John Moore, 49 years old, mother Winny Dill, born South Carolina, drayman, mulatto. Application 3 Jun 1863. Notice given. No objection. Registered July Term 1863 upon oath of Richard J. Pass, Guardian.

Matilda Kelly, 35 years old, mother's name not known, born Augusta, seamstress, mulatto. Application 8 Jun 1863. Notice given. No objection. Registered July Term 1863 upon oath of George W. Lamar, Guardian.

Chloe Ann Dent, 35 years old, mother Nancy Dent, born Augusta, seamstress, mulatto. Application 9 Jun 1863. Notice given. No objection. Registered July Term 1863 upon oath of James Harper. William Philip, Guardian.

Laura Dent, 34 years old, mother Nancy Dent, born Augusta, washer & ironer, mulatto. Application 9 Jun 1863. Notice given. No objection. Registered July Term 1863 upon oath of James Harper. William Philip, Guardian.

Mack Parker, 35 years old, mother Olly Parker, born Augusta, washer & ironer, brown complexion. Application 9 Jun 1863. Notice given. No objection. Registered July Term 1863 upon oath of John A. Bohler, Guardian.

Daniel Lamar, 40 years old, mother Fanny Lamar, born Augusta, carpenter, brown complexion. Application 9 Jun 1863. Notice given. No objection. Registered July Term 1863 upon oath of George W. Lamar.

Jane Brux, 47 years old, mother Betsey Brux, born Augusta, seamstress, mulatto. Application 12 Jun 1863. Notice given. No objection. Registered July Term 1863 upon oath of Charles G. Goodrich. William H. Goodrich, Guardian.

John Barefield, 26 years old, mother Jane Brux, born Augusta, cabinet maker, mulatto. Application 12 Jun 1863. Notice given. No objection. Registered July Term 1863 upon oath of John G. Goodrich. William H. Goodrich, Guardian.

Emily Barefield, 30 years old, mother Jane Brux, born Augusta seamstress, mulatto. Application 12 Jun 1863. Notice given. No objection. Registered July Term 1863 upon oath of John G. Goodrich. William H. Goodrich, Guardian.

Caroline Snowden, 19 years old, mother Jane Brux, born Augusta, seamstress, light mulatto. Application 12 Jun 1863. Notice given. No objection. Registered July Term 1863 upon oath of John G. Goodrich. William H. Goodrich, Guardian.

George B. Snowden, 17 years old, mother Jane Brux, born Augusta, cigar maker, light mulatto. Application 12 Jun 1863. Notice given. No objection. Registered July Term 1863 upon oath of John G. Goodrich. William H. Goodrich, Guardian.

Louisa Campbell, 22 years old, mother Jane Brux, born Augusta, seamstress, mulatto. Application 12 Jun 1863. Notice given. No objection. Registered July Term 1863 upon oath of John G. Goodrich. William H. Goodrich, Guardian.

Lovey Ann King, 23 years old, mother Elvira King, born Greene County, washer & ironer, mulatto. Application 16 Jun 1863. Notice given. No objection. Registered July Term 1863 upon oath of Albert Webster, Guardian.

John King, 17 years old, mother Elizabeth King, born Greene County, laborer, brown complexion. Application 17 Jun 1863. Notice given. No objection. Registered July Term 1863 upon oath of Andrew J. Davis. William W. Walker, Guardian.

Malinda Lamar, 36 years old, mother Frances Lamar, born Augusta, mantua maker, brown complexion. Application 25 Jun 1863. Notice given. No objection. Registered July Term 1863 upon oath of George W. Lamar.

Lewis Campbell, 23 years old, mother Jane Brux, born Augusta, tinner, mulatto. Application 25 Jun 1863. Notice given. No objection. Registered July Term 1863 upon oath of John G. Goodrich. William H. Goodrich, Guardian.

Richard Lamar, 78 years old, mother Nancy Lamar, born Richmond County, carpenter, black complexion. Application 25 Jun 1863. Notice given. No objection. Registered July Term 1863 upon oath of George W. Lamar.

Thomas Thomas, 50 years old, mother Violet Dillon, born Augusta, saddler, black complexion.

Polly Ann Gantt, 40 years old, mother Betsey Gant, born Columbia County, washer & ironer, mulatto. Application 29 Jun 1863. Notice given. No objection. Registered August Term 1863 on oath of Lewis Lovell. John A. Christian, Guardian.

Rachel Harris, 16 years old, mother Rachel Brister, born Augusta, washer & ironer, brown complexion. Application 29 Jun 1863. Notice given. Continued August Term.

Isaac Harman, 71 years old, Elizabeth Harman, born Richmond County, laborer, mulatto. Application 29 Jun 1863. Notice given. No objection. Registered August term 1863 on oath of William Glendinning, Guardian.

Caroline Melton, 24 years old, mother Elizabeth Melton, born Richmond County, washer & cook, mulatto. Application Jul 1863. Continued August Term 1863. No objection. Registered September Term 1863 on oath of Joseph E. Burch.

Martha Sanders, 25 years old, mother Mary Ann Berry, born South Carolina, nurse, mulatto. Application 13 Oct 1863. No objection. Registered November Term 1863 on oath of Mrs. Love Hester.

Index

Alonzo, 123
Augustus, 123
Boston, 14
China, 11
Chloe, 15
Daniel, 18
Edmund, 16
Emma, 123
H. H., 97
Jim, 15
John, 15, 105
Joy, 15
Lewis, 11
Lucinda, 18
Mary Jane, 123
Maryland, 25
Mildred, 124
Nancy, 11, 12
Rachel, 14
Rose, 15
Sam, 16
Sophia, 25
William, 105
Wm. Henry, 124
Aldrich
H., 63
Anthony
D. L., 126
Antony
L., 114
L. L., 105, 109, 111
Oliver, 50, 53
Armond
Augustus, 84
Darias, 83, 84
Qu___, 84
Quilly, 84
Sarah Jane, 84
William, 84
Bacon
Eugene, 14
Bahler
Jno. A., 134

Banyer
Mary, 128
Barber
F. C., 111, 115
Barefield
Emily, 144, 149
John, 144, 149
W. Henry, 126
William Henry, 138
Barnes
W. E., 125, 129, 132
Wm. E., 116, 117
Barrot, 12
Betty, 11, 12
Lucy, 11, 12
Barton
W., 19
Beall
Martha, 128
Mary, 141
Bell
H. D., 113, 120, 127, 132
Benefield
Emily, 112
Benefold
James, 98
Beneful, 61, 63
Benning
Frances, 134, 138
Hannah, 137
Hensley, 134, 141
Jim, 134, 139
Rosetta, 138, 139, 141
Simon, 134
William, 134, 137
Berry
Mary Ann, 145, 151
Bignan
Cloe, 33
Bignon
Cloe, 42
Bing
Priscilla, 27, 75
Black

Shadrack, 41
Cadle
  Arch, 134
Calvin
  T. J., 112, 117, 120, 121, 131
  Thos. J., 106, 109, 111
Campbell
  George, 43
  Lewis, 144, 150
  Louisa, 144, 150
  Sambo, 23
Carnes
  Elizabeth, 68, 82, 96, 103
  F., 56, 58
  Francis, 54, 68, 82, 96, 103
  Isaiah, 142
  Isiah, 106, 115
  Jack, 33, 35, 41, 45, 50, 72
  James, 35, 39, 45, 49, 68, 82, 96, 103
  Jas., 54, 56, 58
  Joe, 33, 35, 41, 46, 72
  John, 131, 142
  Josiah, 129
  Julus, 120
  L., 56
  Lucy, 32, 35, 39, 45, 49, 53, 58, 68, 82,
    96, 103, 120
  Mary Ann, 45
  Mathew, 106, 115, 129, 142
  Sarah, 31, 35, 39, 45, 49, 53, 56, 58, 68,
    80, 82, 96, 103, 106, 115, 142
  Simeon, 68, 80
  Simuel, 106, 115, 129, 142
  V., 56
  Varna, 58
  Viana, 49, 53
  Viena, 129
  Vienna, 32, 35, 39, 45, 68, 80, 106, 115,
    142
  Wm., 32
Carns
  Jack, 22
  Joe, 22
  Lucy, 22
  Sarah, 22
  Vienna, 22

Caroline
  Daniel, 25, 34
  Danl., 19
  Jeremiah, 70
  Marheed, 34
  Martisia, 70
Carter
  John B., 147
  Lewis, 44
  Thomas, 22, 30, 53
  Tom, 39, 46, 49
  Willis, 31, 50
  Williss, 26
Casey
  Shadrack, 46, 52
Catlin
  Charles, 107
  Chas., 128
  L. L., 133
Cecile
  Mary Ann, 96
  William, 96
Charles
  Cecile, 84, 96
Chavers
  Edmund, 35, 42, 59, 85
  John, 77
  Laura, 85
  Rachael, 25, 35, 42, 59, 85
  Rachel, 54
Chaves
  Edmd., 54
Chavons
  Fairee, 139
Chisholm
  Sarah, 135
Christian
  J. A., 113, 116, 125, 131, 133
  Jno. A., 115, 134
  John A., 150
Chritian
  J. A., 127
Clark, 17
  Ellen, 117, 126, 137
  U. B., 63
Clarke

154

158

159

Barton, 116
  Frances, 116
Martin
  Bob, 24, 29, 39, 46, 49, 54, 56, 58, 72
  Elizabeth, 73
  James, 72
  M. R., 63
  Nancy, 72
Mastin
  L. C., 117
Mathews
  Ira D., 147
Maxwell
  James R., 139, 147
  Leah, 139, 147
  Rebecca, 137
McC.
  Wm., 104
McCormick
  Wm., 101
McFarland
  Betsey, 74
McFarlane
  Betsy, 41, 73
McGan
  Philip, 97
McKinn, 26
McLaws
  W. R., 117
  Wm. R., 97
M'Clendon
  Betsy, 11
  Harry, 11
  Jacob, 11
  Kesiah, 11
  Rose, 11
McMurphy
  J. E., 121
Melton
  Caroline, 145, 151
  Elizabeth, 145, 151
Meriwether
  Richard, 11, 12
Millen
  David, 73
  James, 73

  Jane, 73
  Mary Ann, 73
  Polly, 72
  Richard, 73
  Virginia, 73
Miller
  A. G., 108
  A. J., 101, 103
  Andrew J., 102
  F. H., 120, 128
  J. M., 131
  Jane, 18
  Jno. M., 124
  Jonathan, 104, 115
  T. W., 121
M'Lean
  Andrew, 11
Moats
  Jane, 137
Monroe
  John, 40, 51, 77
  Lewis, 26, 51
  Louis, 40
  Maria, 40, 51, 76, 77
  Mariah, 22, 36
  Mary, 40, 51, 76
  William Henry, 77
Moon
  Isabella, 72
Moore
  Amelia, 136, 147
  Hannah Jones, 66
  Isabella, 82, 132, 139
  Jane, 102, 107, 112
  Jeffrey, 72, 82
  John, 143, 149
  Joshua, 11
  Mary A., 66
  Mary Ann Jones, 66
  Mary Elizabeth, 102
Morrison
  D., 63
Mullen
  Mary, 60
Mullin
  Betsey, 27

Munroe
  Mariah, 32
Muskey
  J., 98
Narius
  Daniel, 117, 126
Nelson
  J., 132
  John, 107
Nurris
  Daniel, 137
O'Neil
  Joshua, 131
Oliver
  J. H., 127
  S. H., 120, 125
Osmond
  Jesse, 104
  Mary, 141
Pace
  Thomas, 38
Page
  John, 77
  Mariah, 22
  Mary, 76
  William Henry, 77
Paris
  Tom, 29, 37
Parish
  G., 118
  G. F., 96, 108, 109, 111
  Garey F., 103
  Gary F., 98, 106, 107
  Geo., 115, 116, 124
  Gerry F., 102
Parker
  Adaline, 115, 126
  Ally, 144
  Mack, 144, 149
  Olly, 149
Parks
  Betsey, 143
  Hannah, 137
  James, 106, 115, 143
  Judy, 106, 115
Parris

Thomas, 54
Tom, 39, 47, 49, 56
Pass
  Richard J., 149
Payne
  Elizabeth, 140, 147
Penn
  T. H., 31
Persons
  T. F., 105
Philip
  William, 149
Phinizy
  J., Sr., 132
  Jno., 103, 115
  Jno., Jr., 117, 119, 120
  John, 96
  Robert N., 147
Pleasant
  Madison, 114
  Margaret, 114
  Mary Frances, 114
  Sarah Eliza, 114
Pleasants
  Madison, 127
  Margaret, 127, 143
  Martha Ann, 127
  Mary Frances, 127
  Sarah, 127
Poisson
  Jane, 141
  Urselle, 25
Pope
  A., 55
  Alec, 47, 52
  Alex, 75
  Alleck, 41
  Aluk, 30
Posa
  Elizabeth, 84
Posner
  David, 10
  Joseph Gabriel, 10
  Silvia, 10
Poutler
  Nehemiah K., 148

164

www.ingramcontent.com/pod-product-compliance
Lightning Source LLC
Chambersburg PA
CBHW061742270326
41928CB00011B/2345